ANDALUSIAN
ROCK CLIMBS

John and Oliver Addy, on a windy Walkway.
The stuff that nightmares are made of

ANDALUSIAN ROCK CLIMBS

including TENERIFE

An Introductory Guide
by
Chris Craggs

CICERONE PRESS
MILNTHORPE, CUMBRIA

© Chris Craggs 1992
ISBN 1 85284 109 5
British Library Cataloguing-in-Publication Data. A catalogue record for
this book is available from the British Library.

ACKNOWLEDGEMENTS

Thanks to the many people who have given me encouragement
with this guide both off and on the rock. To Chris Williams, who first
suggested the area was worth a visit, to Mike and Elaine Owen, Phil
Davidson, Pete and Cara Blackburn, John and Oliver Addy, Dave
and Bill Gregory, Colin Binks, Mike Appleton, Chris Hindley and
Nigel Baker. To the Howards who always treated us like long lost
friends and lastly to Sherri Davy who left the beach to suffer the
horrors of the Walkway and hardly complained at all.

Advice to Readers

Readers are advised that whilst every effort is taken by the author
to ensure the accuracy of this guidebook, changes can occur
which may affect the contents. It is advisable to check locally on
transport, accommodation, shops etc but even rights-of-way can
be altered and, more especially overseas, paths can be eradicated
by landslip, forest fires or changes of ownership.

The publisher would welcome notes of any such changes

Front Cover: *Colin Binks on LOS MUYAYOS, 6b+ (E4 6a) El Corral,
1st November 1991. Where were you, the Costa Blanca?*

Back Cover: *Chris Craggs on GUIRI 6c (E4 6a) at Las Canadas, Tenerife. The
volcano El Tiede (12,172ft) makes a superb backdrop*

CONTENTS

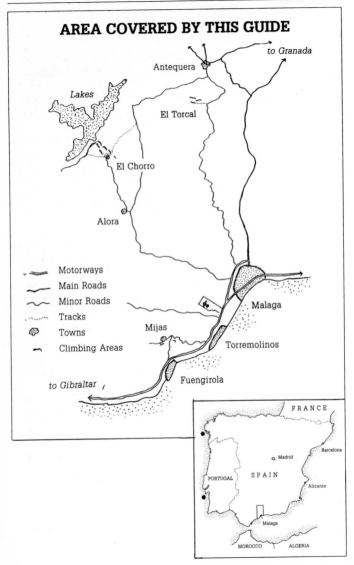

INTRODUCTION

Southern Spain is a land of stark contrasts. The Costa del Sol (coast of sunshine) presents mile upon mile of superb beaches backed by mile upon mile of concrete. Lack of any coherent planning has led to ribbon development on a quite amazing scale and the despolation of what must once have been a magnificent coastline. The urban squalor that surrounds many of the larger towns comes as a real shock to our northern European sensibilities but Andalusia is the poorest province in Spain and many of the locals are more concerned with earning enough to survive than keeping the place tidy.

A short distance inland are rolling hills and open farmland of true Andalusia, small white villages pepper the countryside and there is a whole different life-style. This is 'real' Spain, where it is not uncommon to see donkeys used for transport and oxen for ploughing the land. Many people still live in poverty and English is rarely spoken. The life-style here has changed little in the last fifty years and the cult of 'Mañana' continues to rule the people.

Also inland are the major cities of Cordoba, Seville and Granada. These are settlements on a grand scale based on ancient Moorish towns and with many fine buildings surviving to this day. They are worth a visit if you fancy a day off and want to do the Culture Vulture bit. Between these cities and the coast are scattered many small towns, compact communities that huddle together in a way that is a reminder that this area has seen more than its fair share of unrest over the centuries.

To the east the Sierra Nevada rise to 3,482 metres (11,317 feet) in the peak of Mulhacen and skiing is available here throughout most winters. A good break from the climbing can be had by travelling to Granada and on to the resort of Solynieve (an easy 3 hours from El Chorro or Malaga) for a couple of days on the piste! A good variety of reasonably priced accommodation is available in Granada and on the road up to the slopes. Ski equipment can be hired at the resort and a day pass costs about 3,000pts, though be warned, the weekends can be very busy.

The area described in the guide is so far south (Malaga is only 120km from the North African coast) that the winters are exceptionally mild. As befits a true Mediterranean climate it does rain in the winter though short heavy showers tend to be the pattern, and much of the rock dries very quickly. Any time between October and April you would be unlucky not to get as much time on the rock as your hands could take.

The Guide

This book describes a collection of foreign rock climbs in a very British format. I have given accurate details, stars, E grades and technical grades where possible, together with the Spanish equivalents, and tried to make the guide "readable" as well as adding the odd touch of humour. The Spanish grades are mostly taken from the topo at the Station Bar (at the lower entrance to the gorge at El Chorro - a focal point for local climbers), from Spanish magazines and from conversations with the locals, I take no responsibility for these. I have also given UK grades for all routes up to a 7a Spanish, and these are from a consensus where one exists though I take full responsibility for the grades. Wherever there is doubt about a grade I have erred on the side of over grading rather than under grading. That does not mean that the guide is full of 'soft touches', but I would rather give someone a pleasant surprise than a nasty shock!

WHY BOTHER TO INCLUDE UK GRADES?

To do sport climbs regularly in Britain you really need to be operating at 7a (E5 6a) or above. Most people who climb up to the middle Extreme grades will not have experienced real sport climbing unless they have already visited the continent and so the dual grades will offer a chance to get the feel of the system, though with any attempt at comparisons there are bound to be anomalies. It always makes for pub talk.

Some may argue that a topo guide would serve the area just as well but I believe that the majority of British climbers enjoy having a guide to browse through, to get inspired by and not least of all to tick off. If you only have a week's climbing most people want to be led to the best routes with the minimum of hassle, and that is what this guide tries to do. If you want a real adventure, it is quite possible to do without any guide and go off to do your own thing.

There is a fairly rudimentary topo guide kept in the Station Bar which is updated regularly with recent developments if you run out of things to do.

The Climbing

The amount of rock available for climbing throughout this area is considerable but development has been at best somewhat erratic. Even on the most popular crags there are obvious gaps that have been ignored and major lines that with a little cleaning would be low grade classics in the UK. Usually the cleanest and most accessible rock is climbed on and everything else is ignored.

By far the best known area is El Chorro and this is the ideal place to base yourself (see Where To Stay, below). Here a river and a railway cut through a spectacular gorge. The river has created the cliffs with the railway and its attendant Walkway providing access to them. This railway (the main line from Malaga to Cordoba and Seville) is doubtless the reason that the area was developed in the first place. Local climbers are able to catch regular and cheap trains from the centre of Malaga to within 10 minutes walk of the climbing, spend a day on the rocks, have a few beers at the Station Bar and then catch a train back home at the end of a satisfying day out.

At El Chorro there is a considerable variety of climbing both in grade and style with a remarkable number of high grade climbs. The Cotos provides fine slab pitches, not all of which are easy, Los Venenos offers "plonk on" face climbing and the Invento and Makinodromo have some really steep pitches. Pocket pulling is available on several of the cliffs and big leads are the speciality of El Polverin.

Mijas is very much an outcrop with short fierce and very safe pitches and El Torcal presents acres of rock in a high and wild setting with an unusual style of climbing because of the erosion the rock has suffered.

In all the areas described in this book the vast majority of the protection and all the belays are fixed and substantial. There are none of the death trap single corroding caving bolts that have masqueraded as main belays on Pen Trwyn, or the rotting pegs that are supposed to protect pitches in the Avon Gorge. On some of the lower grade climbs the fixed bolts can be rather spaced and a selection of mid range and large wire is useful. Despite this minor inconvenience, if nuts are required you can guarantee that the placements are obvious and 'bomber'. There is none of the good old gripping British tradition; poor wires in dubious placements, RPs that fall out as you climb past them or secret runner slots that only the initiated are aware of. On the harder routes the gear is fixed and solid almost without exception. Many of the pitches are longer than twenty-five metres and so double ropes are needed to effect a convenient retreat. Paired ring bolts or wire cable with large steel rings are the commonest belays at the top of the climbs and these allow easy retrieval of the ropes.

How To Get There

Malaga is the airport for all the resorts on the Costa del Sol, Fuengirola, Marbella, and Torremolinos the most infamous of these. In the summer season literally millions of sun-seekers pour in for their week sizzling on the beach, and a night life consisting mostly of expensive discos, cheap booze and chips. This has led to the over development of the coast line but at least it offers the discerning climber cheap flights to an area with reliable winter weather and enough rock to guarantee a couple of good weeks rocking. There are reasonably priced flights from all regional airports and a little shopping around using phone numbers from the Sunday papers or the television's Ceefax service may well pay dividends. Many of the flights to Malaga are on Sundays which can be rather inconvenient but is much better than staying at home! Once in Malaga there are a couple of options on how to get to El Chorro if indeed that is where you intend to stay.

A car is not essential in this area as long as you intend to stop at El Chorro though having access to 'wheels' is certainly extremely useful for getting around, visiting other areas and doing the shopping! Cars are best booked from the UK before you leave. At all costs avoid booking a car at the airport - figures of up to £600 a week are not unheard of. If you do arrive without a car and then decide you need one, try one of the small companies along the coast.

I have always used PREMIER CAR HIRE who are based in Harlow and who have a depot at Malaga airport. They have always proved reliable and the smaller cars are especially good value. There is usually a rep who will meet you with the keys (don't forget your driving licence) at any hour of the day or night, and such items as roof racks and child seats are fitted free of charge. The car comes with a full tank of gas which you pay for at the airport, then you return it as near empty as you dare! Winter rates start at about £75 a week (not bad split 4 ways!). A price brochure can be obtained by ringing 0279 641040.

If you do not intend or cannot afford to hire a car there is a cheap and regular underground train service from the airport into the centre of Malaga, arriving next to the main railway station. There are regular trains from here (see Appendix) to Alora and El Chorro.

To get to El Chorro by car follow the road out of the airport and turn left (east) along the coastal motorway towards Malaga. Within a couple of kilometres the road crosses a river, the Guadalhorce, that also runs through the gorge at El Chorro. Turn off right here and pass under the motorway to reach a road heading inland and passing through an industrial estate (the beauty of Spain). This is followed keeping left at any junctions for four kilometres to a T junction opposite the chemical works. Turn left and follow the rather tortuous road through Campanillas, Estacion de Cartama and Pizarra. Five kilometres after the last of these a left turn crosses the valley and rises up the hill to the spectacularly situated town of Alora. Turn right at the first set of traffic lights and follow the road for twelve kilometres finally to cross the impressive dam into El Chorro. About one hour (fifty-five km) from the airport.

Where To Stay

There are a number of options available as far as accommodation goes depending on the size of your purse and the style of holiday you are intent on having.

It is possible to rent apartments cheaply on the coast in the tourist low season but this is a little inconvenient if you intend to climb regularly at El Chorro because of the hour or so drive to get there. If on the other hand you are having a family holiday with a bit of climbing thrown in stopping on the coast may be the ideal

11

solution. Fuengirola has a variety of cheap accommodation and the added advantage the Mijas is only ten minutes drive away; expect to pay c.£10 a night for a double room with shower and cooking facilities.

Opposite the railway station in Malaga there are a considerable number of cheap hostels and hotels, as well as a selection of restaurants and cafes. Stopping here and catching the train each day 360pts or about £2 return) is a viable proposition. The journey takes an hour. Alternatively there are a number of cheap pensions and hotels in Alora, which is 15 kilometres from El Chorro; you should expect to pay about £10-£12 a night for a double room. The train from here to El Chorro is 130pts (70p) for a day return.

In El Chorro itself there is the Bar Gargantua opposite the station which has pleasant rooms (no real cooking facilities) for about £8 per person per night. The prices are fairly variable, markedly more expensive at holiday times and when it is raining! If there is a group of you then it might be worth trying a bit of negotiation. It is worth pointing out at this juncture that El Chorro cannot be described as a resort by any stretch of the imagination. One Horse Town would be a better description, but it is a great place to get away from it all!

Free camping is possible at El Chorro (and El Torcal) and is very popular with the Spanish. The two favoured places are in the trees at the end of the road opposite Albercones or amongst the orange groves across the river from the foot of the Cotos. The first of these options has the advantage that if you have a car it can be driven to the campsite. The second option requires a 20-minute walk with the camping gear but offers a campsite in superb isolation, and a real chance to get to know the countryside. There is water and a small toilet block available at the station. In early 1992 one of the local climbers was in the process of setting up a campsite and refugio below Las Encantadas; take the first right turn after the cliff to check this out.

There are also civilised campsites available by the lakes at the top end of the gorge, (Parques Adales) though a car is definitely needed if you decide to stop there. There are bars, shops, beaches and boat hire, what more could a man desire.

Just outside El Chorro (five minutes walk) there are some self-catering cottages and flats owned by an English family, Mr & Mrs Howard, who live nearby. There are six cottages sleeping between two and five people and they cost approximately £30 per person per week in the winter season and about £40 from Easter through the summer. Availability and further details can be obtained by phoning Mrs Bell who handles the booking in England on 081 998 0381. There have already been occasions of climbers booking places and then filling them with friends sleeping on the floor. The owners are understandably not too happy at this development and it would be a pity if this useful accommodation was lost to climbers because of the selfish actions of a few individuals.

A recent development is the Hostal El Chorro situated 30 miles north-west of El Chorro. For between £150 and £180 a week the owners will collect you and your team from the airport, feed you, give you bunkhouse-style accommodation, deliver you to the cliffs each day and even show you where specific routes are located, good value and definitely holidaying without tears? For further information, booking forms etc. phone Sandra Belcham on 0873 856682.

SHOPPING

There are two small shops in El Chorro, though neither of them is particularly easy to find despite the tiny size of the place. If you fail to locate them try collaring one of the local children and trying out your Spanish: "Donde esta el mercado, por favor?"

They are usually more than willing to help. Both shops stock most of daily requirements except for fresh meat, including beer and gas canisters. Prices are quite high and it is well worth considering driving down to Alora to stock up. There are several small supermarkets on the right as you approach Alora from El Chorro, and shopping here should cut your bills by up to 40%. Driving into Alora is to be avoided at all costs as it is a maze of steep, narrow roads: park on the outskirts and walk in.

There are two vans that visit El Chorro every day, stopping at the station and selling fresh bread and vegetables. Prices are reasonable.

If you visit the coast, Malaga or Mijas, there are many hypermarkets which sell everything at very reasonable prices.

Again it may be worth stocking up.

Finally there are a couple of climbing shops in Malaga on the Calle de Carreteria (north of the city centre) that are worth a visit if you are in town, though don't forget the siesta. They have a reasonable stock of equipment and boots are especially cheap, perhaps 50% of their price in the UK with cash being the preferred form of exchange.

El Camino del Rey or the King's Way

Perhaps the single most spectacular feature of the gorge at El Chorro is the King's Way, a narrow catwalk attached to the cliff face, in places two hundred feet above the waters of the Guadalhorce. It was built in the 1920s to offer access to workmen who were employed in the construction of a hydroelectric scheme through the gorge. Large sections of the Walkway are in a poor state of repair at present though there are talks about the possibility of renovating it to its former solidity to act as a tourist attraction. If you are wondering how it got into its present state watch the last few minutes of the film *Von Ryans Express* and all will be revealed! As it stands (or should that read 'as long as it stands') the trip through the upper and lower gorges along the Walkway is a truly memorable one. A head for heights and a certain steadiness are required as a fall from 99% of the catwalk would definitely prove fatal. In a couple of the very hairiest sections wire cables have been bolted to the wall so that it is possible to safeguard yourself by clipping on to them as with the 'via ferratas' of the Alps. This requires the wearing of a harness and is a good idea unless you have supreme confidence in your foot work.

The walk through the gorge takes a leisurely two to three hours and is a great way of getting to know the layout of the various cliffs as well as getting a feel for the area. It is best done from 'top to bottom', this having the advantage of being gently downhill and of finishing at the Station Bar. It requires either being dropped off, or leaving the car at the top and collecting it later, or perhaps doing a 'cross over' with another team.

Records for running or mountain biking the Walkway should be sent to the Guinness Book of Ridiculous Feats.

THE KING'S WAY ******* Easy to E5 (depending on your head for heights) 4km

Start from the hydroelectric power station which is reached by a nine-kilometre drive from El Chorro (see LAS BANERAS Access). Pass round the side of the fence and follow a descending path round the left side of the buildings to reach a level track leading to the old gate and memorial plaque. (True heroes in high summer might want to consider descending to and following the river through the base of the gorge. Now that really would be a trip and half!)

Pass through the gateway and be instantly stunned by the setting, the quality of the rock and the brilliant-looking climbs on the other side of the rift. After neck-craning and whooping a bit continue through as the gorge gradually opens out. At one point a set of steps descends to a lower level and these are worth a quick explore if time is not too pressing. Here the massive walls directly above and on the opposite side of the gorge are worth an ogle at - impressive.

The Walkway now descends to reach the level of the channel that was cut to carry the water to the generating station below the lower gorge and the rim of this gives a pleasant balancing act. If you decide to fall it is best to aim to the right into the channel rather than to the left where the drop is rather larger.

After a short uphill section (major roof climbs for the year 2010) the path rounds a bend to find a decrepit bridge spanning a 150-foot deep mini ravine. This is LES PETIT DESFILADERO, the home of a series of tough routes reached by abseil. Crossing the bridge (at a steady trot) gives access to the railway line and a soft option to the next rather more gripping section of the Walkway. The railway line can be followed all the way back to the station through a series of eight tunnels.

To continue with the trip follow the Walkway around a buttress into a position of some exposure. There is no handrail and there is the odd hole in the floor so a modicum of care is required before a final 'hairy' section leads back to terra firma.

Now a level section of path is followed for a kilometre or so along the line of the old water channel, with great views of the various cliffs on the other side of the valley. For those who have found the whole experience thus far a bit of a gripper, now is the time to descend to the river and wade across to scramble up the other side and gain the safety of the railway line.

For those who are made of sterner stuff continue round to where the Walkway restarts as the gorge starts to close in again. A short scramble leads onto it then a couple of 'missing' sections are passed without incident and the path runs out around a leaning arête (see frontispiece). This section is easy but scary especially if a strong wind is blowing, in which case crossing it doggie fashion might not be a bad idea. The Walkway continues round a large bay (EL RECORDO), and out round an arête into a narrower bay, it is worth noting the way that the whole Walkway has pulled away from the wall on this section, hmmm. This next bay is spanned by a spindly concrete bridge, and running or all fours may be deemed appropriate again. Just around the next corner is the aptly named Pipe Bridge spanning the gorge and crossed by the footpath.

A LITTLE DIVERSION

From just above the start of the Pipe Bridge a thick wire cable spans the gorge diagonally in a massive arc to the buttress taken by ZEPPELIN. The crossing of this, by whatever means, would be a wild, wild trip, just thinking about it is enough to bring you out into a major sweat.

NOTE: I have heard unsubstantiated rumours that the crossing has been made - but is it true?

Back to the reality. Cross the Pipe Bridge and go round a corner to be met by the crux. Here a piece of railway line spans a ten-foot gap where the Walkway has been completely removed by a rock fall. Shimmy across this with great aplomb or quake across it in total terror (and with your eyes shut) to reach the sanctuary of solid concrete then amble on with a growing sense of self-satisfaction. The railway line is three minutes away and the Station Bar another fifteen minutes pleasant stroll. It must be time for a cool beer, go to it, and don't forget to raise a glass to the King...

Nigel Baker enjoying the technicalities of
MOCOS DE HIERRO 6b (E3 6A), Los Venenos

EL CHORRO

As mentioned in the introduction to this book El Chorro is the most important climbing centre covered by this guide, and is presently the most important centre in all of southern Spain. Here there exists a vast selection of routes across a broad range of difficulty and with an immense amount of rock still to go at. A few longer climbs have been put up, ZEPPELIN being the most important of these at 1,100 feet long.

The area is basically a large gorge with a river and railway running through it. The upper and lower section of the gorge are narrow and impressive, whereas the central section is open and quite sublime.

The individual cliffs are described separately as they are approached from the village of El Chorro and in the order that they are met walking up the gorge. There are two parking places that are most convenient for these approaches.

1. From immediately in front of the Station Bar a narrow road rises over a hump, passes through the houses and heads off into the woods. At the end of this there is plenty of parking (and camping) space opposite the small cliff of ALBERCONES. All the other approaches are described from here.

2. A slightly shorter but steeper walk in is possible by driving along the tarmacked road that runs along the eastern side of the reservoir (the same side as the village) to a parking place below and impressive bridge carrying the railway line. A rough track leads up leftwards to reach the railway line between the first two tunnels on the regular approach. This approach is useful after rain when the regular track becomes extremely slippery.

The easiest approach to reach the climbing in the Upper Gorge, (LAS BANERAS and LES PETIT DESFILADERO) is to drive across the dam at El Chorro and turn right. The rough road is followed

Pitch 2 of LA DAMA DEL VIENTO 6b Africa

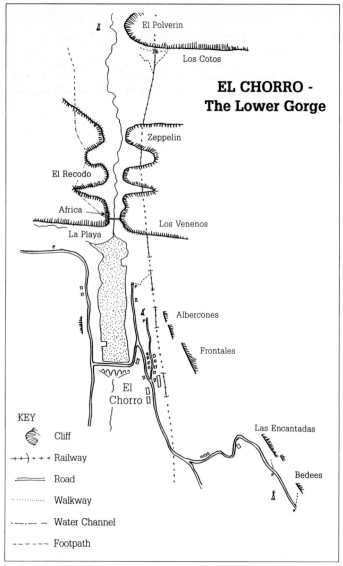

El Polverin

Los Cotos

**EL CHORRO -
The Lower Gorge**

Zeppelin

El Recodo

Africa

Los Venenos

La Playa

Albercones

Frontales

El
Chorro

Las Encantadas

Bedees

KEY

Cliff

+++)+++ Railway

Road

.... Walkway

.—.—.— Water Channel

------ Footpath

uphill for six kilometres to an impressive junction. Turn right and after two kilometres turn right again onto a dirt track, just before a bar. Follow this first uphill then down through a tunnel to a parking area in front of the gates of the hydroelectric power station. Pass round the fence and follow a path round to the left of the buildings. LAS BANERAS is two minutes away and LES PETIT DESFILADERO is another ten minutes beyond that.

The first cliff to be described lies a short distance to the south of the village of El Chorro set high above the valley.

LAS ENCANTADAS

Character

A superb south-facing crag in an open and truly beautiful setting. The rock varies from perfect grey "goutte d'eaued" limestone, through sections of flowstone, to steep red pocketed walls, and the outlook over the orange and lemon orchards of the Guadalhorce valley is sublime. Development of the cliff is at a stage where there are still plenty of lines and even whole sections of cliff to go at, get a battery-powered drill on your Christmas list before it is too late! Access is simple and protection is (almost) invariably both frequent and sound. The right side of the cliff has some superb-looking leaning pocketed walls that are completely undeveloped at the moment, criminal.

NOTE: I wrote the above introduction in March 1991 and on a return visit four weeks later, working on this guide, many of the lines had already been bolted. There is still plenty of rock to go at but you will have to get a move on! Possible new route activity should be borne in mind when using the guide on this cliff.

Access

From the station at El Chorro follow the dirt road east past the Bar Gargantua, and up the hill beyond. Keep left at the first junction and continue steeply until the road begins to flatten out below the prominent red cliff. Limited parking is available on the right a short distance past the cliff and a vague path leads up left to the foot rock, two minutes away. This is twenty minutes steep walk, or five minutes easy drive from the station. Please keep off any cultivated land here, the locals are not wealthy folks.

The routes are described from left to right.

To the left of the impressive main wall is an area of more broken rock with a tree in front of it. Left of this is a short subsidiary buttress with a clean lower wall and beyond this a grassy gully and a smaller buttress, steep at the bottom and easing in angle as it rises. This leftmost piece of rock contains one central line.

BOLANDRO 6a+ (E1 5c) 40ft

Difficult moves on sharp and spikey holds lead up the lower wall past two bolts. Once the slab is reached much easier climbing leads to the lowering anchors. Not really one of Spain's great routes.

NOMBRE PROPIO * 6a (E1 5b) 40ft

The left side of the subsidiary buttress is a short pocketed rib containing four bolts. A tricky start gains good pocket holds then a series of sustained moves lead to a final awkward stretch up and right to reach the chains. A more entertaining pitch than first appearances might suggest.

To the right are three bolt lines running up steep pocketed rock and onto grey slabs, whilst further to the right is a line marked by two threads.

BOHEM D'ESTRELL * 6b (E1 5b) 50ft

The left-hand line is quite steep but the holds are good and the bolts are plentiful; great sport, relish it because like all good things in life it is over far too soon.

POUM POUM RAN RAN * 6b (E1 5b) 50ft

The central bolt ladder has a leaning start which is climbed on excellent but well-spaced pockets (5c for dwarfs?) by powerful moves to gain the much more amenable slab above. Romp on to the lowering bolts.

PARA QUE DISFRUTE LA GANAYAR ** 6a (E2 5c) 50ft

A pleasant piece of exercise up a shallow leaning groove in the centre of the subsidiary buttress. The name is painted on the rock. The initial groove is bridged with good pocketed handholds until it is possible to move out right with difficulty to reach good layaways. Gaining the slab above is awkward, then marginally easier climbing on fine grey rock leads to the chains.

CRISIS DE IDENTIDAD * 5+ (E1 5b) 50ft

To the right of the groove of the last route is a bulging wall containing two well-spaced thread runners and an iron rod at foot

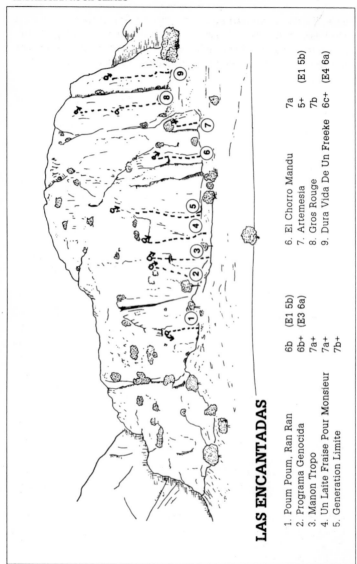

LAS ENCANTADAS

1. Poum Poum, Ran Ran	6b	(E1 5b)	
2. Programa Genocida	6b+	(E3 6a)	
3. Manon Tropo	7a+		
4. Un Laite Fraise Pour Monsieur	7a+		
5. Generation Limite	7b+		

6. El Chorro Mandu	7a		
7. Artemesia	5+	(E1 5b)	
8. Gros Rouge	7b		
9. Dura Vida De Un Freeke	6c+	(E4 6a)	

level. Butch moves lead up to and past the first thread (don't look too closely at the knot). The slab above gives easier climbing and the potential of a ground fall (unless you are carrying a Rock 4) before the second thread is clipped. Move easily left to the belay of the previous route and lower off.

Across a grassy gully and behind a tree that provides welcome shade from the midday sun is the start of the main wall of the cliff. On its left edge is a narrow buttress, steepening as it rises and sporting closely spaced bolts.

ATENEA ** 4 (VS 4b) 60ft

The rather scrappy-looking rib provides a pleasant pitch on good holds especially where the whole thing steepens up. The frequency of the bolts means that the route is a viable lead for the climber who has just had a six-month lay off. There are absolutely no excuses for failing on this one.

There is plenty of good quality unclimbed rock above the belay for those with a sense of adventure and a rack of nuts, otherwise lower off.

PROGRAMA GENOCIDA *** 6b+ (E3 6a) 70ft

A fine pitch up the smooth grey rib bounding the left side of the main wall. Small holds and delicate moves lead up to the third bolt from where the crux sequence leads out right. Step back left and follow the steepening line with sustained interest to a final couple of tricky moves to the chains. The bolts on this pitch appear to have been placed by a climber who was 6ft 3ins tall!

MANON TROPO *** 7a+ 90ft

A great pitch up the rugged wall and over the flat overhang on the left side of the main wall.

An easy start leads to ledges, then press on with escalating difficulties as the angle increases. Small sharp holds lead to a rest below the roof which is passed by a long stretch for a drilled pocket (tut). This move appears to have been 'created' by the same guy who placed the bolts on the previous route, and shorties may find it impossible. Sustained moves on further drilled pockets (tut tut) lead to the chains.

23

*Elaine Owen on PARA QUE DISFRUTE LA GANAYAR 6a (E2 5c),
Las Encantadas*

To the right is a square-cut cave in the base of the cliff. Just left of this is the start of a stunning pitch.

LAS MULAS COMEN MUCHOS CUERDOS *** 8a+ 100ft

Trend left up the leaning wall following a superbly subtle line of tuffa pillars and flowstone rippled rock via fingery and highly technical climbing. Continue steeply over two sets of overhangs to reach belays where the angle finally relents.

To the right of the square-cut cave a closely spaced line of insitu pegs runs up the leaning wall. These could provide exercise for old timers on wet days and a project for rock jocks on hot ones.

To the right again and just beyond the centre of the wall are two fine pitches. Both start from a ledge 10 feet up. The left-hand line sports the newest bolts and is:

UN LAIT FRAISE POUR MONSIEUR *** 7a+ 90ft

Another fine pitch up an unlikely looking section of cliff. Trend left up scoops and bulges on very rough rock and the occasional good pocket hold to the bulges that cross the upper section of the cliff. Breeze over these to the belays which lie a short distance above.

Just to the right is a steep crack line leading to a shallow groove high on the cliff and containing old bolts and pegs. This gives a fine, sustained and long pitch. Carry a few mid range wires (three to six) to supplement the insitu protection.

GENERATION LIMITE *** 7b+ 160ft

From a bolt belay on ledges follow the long pocketed crack line with sustained difficulty passing bolts and the odd peg runner until it is possible to gain into the groove in the upper wall. This is still sustained and delicate to boot and leads to a final steepening, swing left and then follow the arête to the belay. A sensational pitch. Abseil descent.

The right side of the wall is characterised by a series of steep grooves. The leftmost of these is unclimbed at present but would doubtless be a well glossed limestone classic in the UK.

The left wall of the next (central) corner to the right is crossed diagonally by:

25

BUENO BONITO BARRATO ** 6c (E4 6a) 80ft

From the foot of the corner groove climb up and out left onto the wall (or approach direct) which gives a sustained series of moves and spaced bolts until it is possible to swing left (crux) and climb more easily into an overhung bay. Do battle with the roof of this to reach the belays, the angle is steep but thankfully the holds are generous.

The corner system is climbed by:

CANCION PARASORDES * 6a+ (E3 6a) 80ft

A nice pitch rather spoilt by the fact that you have to place your own protection throughout, how very uncivilised. The groove gives sustained steep climbing over a series of overhangs. Scramble up then down to the right or leave some kit and abseil off. If someone did "the right thing" and equipped this route its popularity would be assured.

To the right is a rib with a roof at 50 feet. This is taken by:

EL CHORRO MANDU ** 7b+ 90ft

Climb the rib with continuous interest and a distinct lack of good jugs until below the roof. Power over this (the crux) to reach better holds. Easier climbing leads to the belays just below where the rock turns scrappy. Lower off.

CACEY DECATETO *** 6c+ (E4 6a) 80ft

The shallow right-hand groove gives a great climb, delicate at first and then strenuous and fully equipped with "proper" runners. Bridge the precarious lower section until forced out left onto undercuts close to the previous route. Before strength and confidence evaporate make powerful moves to a world-class finger jam from where a swing right and a couple of powerful pulls should see you hanging from the chains. Lower off.

To the right is a leaning wall peppered with pockets and split by a halfway ledge. This is taken centrally by:

MATIAILLOS LUGARENOS ** E3 6a (6c) 60ft
A steep little beggar on good but sharp and well spaced holds. The upper half of the lower section proves to be the crux and should be tackled centrally but is marginally easier on the left. The halfway ledge proves to be largely illusory and offers only a poor rest before the taxing upper section, what a place to have to start laybacking! The belay lies just above. Perhaps not a good choice for the last route of the day.

To the right a short, narrow buttress forms the end of this section of cliff. This is climbed by:

ARTEMESIA * 5+ (E1 5b) 40ft
The rib is sustained and surprisingly awkward. Thankfully the protection is exemplary...

Around to the right is the large pocketed red wall mentioned in the introduction to this cliff. In early 1991 this was completely undeveloped but by Easter it had a superb selection of tough climbs scattered across it, such is the pace of development. An interesting idea here is the occasional use of bolt on holds to cross "unclimbable" bits of rock. This may not be cricket but it is certainly better than hacking a jug or drilling a pocket. As and when the moves are done free the hold can be replaced by a bolt runner, or the hole simply filled in. Some of the most prominent (and easiest) lines have yet to be climbed.

On the left side of the face is a steep, narrow gully with a highly impressive route on its left wall reached by a tricky scramble. The climb follows an impressive wall and large roof leading to a sharp arête and may be 8a+.

The right wall of the gully has a short grey slab of excellent rock which contains two climbs.

NO PUEDO CONTIDAME * 6c+ (E4 6a) 40ft
The left-hand line has a tricky start which leads to reach good holds, then a thin series of moves eventually reaches a good pocket, sprint on to the belays.

ESPALOA NOMPIADA * 7a+ 50ft
The right-hand line starts off amenably enough then turns mean. A short desperate section gains undercuts from where it is possible to traverse left to the belay of the previous route.

To the right is a large red wall that offers a great selection of climbs and a cracking sunbathing spot at its base.

UN POCO DE VICIO ** 7a+ 80ft
Start by scrambling to the top of the grey pillar on the left side of the wall. Climb the wall leftwards then cross a corner and continue up steeper rock to an impressive bulge. Battle over this to the belays. As the name suggests, a little bit harsh on the hands.

MEZCLA EXPLOSIVA *** 8a 100ft
Start on top of the grey pillar to the right of the previous route. Climb the superb red and grey wall to a large hole at 70 feet. Use the bolt and hold (or do it without and claim it as your prize) to start a difficult sequence to reach better holds which offer steeper climbing to the belays.

The next route starts in the corner to the left of the lowest part of the wall.

KIT GRIMPE *** 7b+ 90ft
Climb straight up the wall on very rough rock to a bay, then trend right and back left to below an overhang. Cross this and use the bolt on 'mono-doigt' to aid moves right to the stance. Lower off or continue up the second pitch of the next route (***).

GROS ROUGE *** 160ft
1.   90ft   7a+   Start at the lowest point of the wall and climb up to reach the left edge of a huge hanging block. Follow the short arête above (or the groove to its right) to reach steeper rock then trend left through bulges to a belay.
2.   70ft   7b   Climb easily up into a large bay then head off up the overhanging wall to difficult moves where the angle starts to drop back. Romp to the belay.

The final route takes a line up the right side of the wall starting at its right edge.

DURA VIDA DE UN FREEKE *** 6c+ (E4 6a) 110ft
A superb sustained pitch. Climb left up the initial slab on small, sharp holds then continue on good but spaced pockets up steeper rock. A couple of thin moves up a bulging rib provide the crux and lead to a gripping runout up the head wall to the belays. The good holds keep arriving, honest.

A couple of hundred yards further along the hillside is a short, domed wall with three worthwhile routes. Please approach this from further up the road and not by crossing the hillside behind the houses.

Bedees

Access
Continue up the road past the main cliff for about half a kilometre to a point where a track branches right to a series of low white buildings (stables?). It is possible to park on the roadside here. The wall with the routes on is hidden from this point but a vague track leads steeply up and left diagonally across the hillside to reach it in five minutes. The routes are quite short but the rock is excellent and the crag is worth visiting, especially in the evening sun, they are described from left to right.

PREPARETE EN LAS BODEGAS * 6b+ (E3 6a) 70ft
The left-hand line gives a sustained pitch that is marked by twinned first bolts. Climb straight up to a bulge that is passed awkwardly then trend right across a scoop with considerable difficulty to the belays. It is possible to avoid the crux by traversing at a higher level. This reduces the grade to (E2 5c) and the lower bulge then provides the crux of the climb.

BEDEES ** 6b (E2 5c) 70ft
A fine pitch sustained and interesting.

29

Start at the foot of the central groove and climb straight up this and the steep slab above, and then on over bulges on superb rock to reach belays shared with the previous route.

EINFACH * 6a+ (E2 6a) 60ft
The right-hand line offers a short but pleasant pitch, starting up a slanting jamming crack and with a thin crux sequence right at the top.

Further to the right some distance up the hillside is a fine and high tower of rock with a red central section. Development of this cliff is in its infancy, though it already contains a fine selection of routes. The cliff is called:

El Corral

Access
Continue up the dirt road past ENCANTADAS and BEDEES until directly below the cliff. There are houses on the right here, with parking on the verge, and with a track doubling back to the left. This is followed (on foot) for 170 metres to where any one of a series of tracks zigzags up through the olive trees to reach the foot of the cliff. Ten minutes from the road.

The routes are described from left to right.

At the left side of the cliff is a massive fallen flake, leading to severely bulging rock. This is tackled by:

ARNOLD ** 7a 80ft
Climb easily to the top of the flake then attack the bulges with conviction. A leaning groove leads to a good flake hold on the left wall which is the launching pad for a monumental leap to the pockets on the lip. Continue up easier but still tilted rock to belays on the right.

To the right is a crack then a neat open shallow groove running up to steeper rock:

EL CORRAL ** 5 (HVS 5b) 60ft

The groove proves to be trickier than first appearances might suggest but offers excellent sustained climbing. At its top follow good holds out right then pull awkwardly onto the slab to reach the belays.

Around to the right is a short pockety crack in the leaning wall, this is:

MANO INCORRECTO ** 6c+ (E4 6b) 60ft

Climb the crack and swing left to a prominent round pocket. Strenuous use of this (crux) gains a niche and gradually easing difficulties before reaching the belays of the previous climb.

To the right are two bolt lines up gently leaning rock. A little talent and a high pain resistance are required for success on the climbs.

LA CANTANTE CALVE *** 7c 70ft

The left-hand line has a good hold (just the one) and some superb sustained climbing.

SUPERMANO *** 7b 70ft

The right-hand line is a little less technical but just as sustained and again of impeccable quality.

LOS MUYAYOS *** 6b+ (E4 6a) 80ft

To the right a thin crack runs up steep rock and onto a fine slab. Start on the left and follow the sustained crack by tough laybacking, then painfully thin finger jamming to reach easier angled rock. Approach the belays direct with delicacy or more easily from the right.

The central section of the cliff consists of a 300-foot high leaning orange wall. It has no free routes on it at present, though an old threaded sling at thirty feet indicates the lines of the original mixed route up the centre of the cliff. There are some plums waiting to be picked here.

In the back right corner of the bay formed by the leaning walls is a substantial enclosure; the corral of the cliffs' name. The right wall of this leans in a truly ridiculous fashion and offers three (or four) desperate test pieces. If you have designs on LOURDES it is probably a wise idea to get a bit of practise in here before you make that long walk up. From left to right the climbs are:

PATA NEGRA *** 8a 70ft
The leftmost line and hanging crack before trending right to the belays.

MONODEDO DE MONO *** 8b 70ft
The central line and radical leaning wall to the same set of belays.

UN DIA DE PLAYA *** 7c+ 70ft
The marginally more reasonable line (the warm up?) starting by the entrance to the Corral and bearing away left to the belay above the last route.

To the right is a long line of bolts up a grossly tilted groove. At present it is a tough project though it already has a name.

CEREGUMIL'S KID *** 8? 90ft
The groove and rib above would appear to require the upper body of a gorilla and the lower body of a ballerina, do you fit the bill?

Climbers on pitches 4 & 5 of ZEPPELIN 6c+ (E4 6a).
Photo: Pete Blackburn

ALBERCONES

Character

The most accessible piece of rock in the area being five seconds from the car and thus guaranteed continuous popularity. This is perhaps not the best place to climb if you can't cope with criticism and "those staring eyes burning into your back" but it is certainly a great place to grab the odd route at the end of the day or when you get that sudden urge! The area is nicknamed the Tennis Courts because of the wire fencing around it and the concrete floor of the left-hand section, though this is in fact a water storage tank of impressive proportions. It offers some short though pleasant pitches on quarried rock directly opposite the car park whilst further to the right the cliff becomes higher, the rock better and the routes rather more worthwhile. The cliff faces south-west and is well sheltered from winds that blow through the gorge.

Towering over the rather diminutive ALBERCONES are some very impressive pieces of good-looking grey rock. All you need is a double rope, a rack of wires and a sense of adventure.

Further to the right running away up the hillside is a series of towering buttresses pierced by large caves and running up to a high castellated ridge. This area is known as FRONTALES. According to the fairly vague topo-guide in the Station Bar this huge cliff contains six routes, up to eight pitches in length and graded from 4 (VS) to about 5+ (E1). At present only one of these (EL AMPTRAX) is fully equipped with insitu runners and this is described below. If you get bored with bolt protected climbing by numbers I am sure a good week's sport is available here.

Access

Immediately in front of the Station Bar a dirt road rises over a mound and passes through the houses before kinking to the right and heading off into the woods. This is followed for just over a kilometre until it ends close to the railway line and to extensive

Sherri Davy on ALUCINOSIS 4 (VS 4c), Los Cotos

parking in the trees. This area is a popular camping spot with the locals and there are almost always a few tents scattered around. The cliff is on the other side of the railway line: Stop, Look and Listen, then run like hell.

The routes are described from left to right.

TRONKOMOUIL 6a (E1 5b) 40ft
The left-hand bolt line is followed on good holds until just below a shallow dirty groove. Move right to a difficult finish up the steep head wall. Single ring bolt belay on the right backed up by a wire cable on the ledge.
Stepping into the scruffy groove reduces the route to HVS 5a and makes it rather pointless.

GANIMEDES * 6b+ (E2 5c/6a) 40ft
Just to the right an awkward start on small holds leads to easier climbing up the wall to a good undercut slot and a resting place. Passing the final bolt is the crux and is distinctly harrowing for the less than average stature climber, though taller ones can span out left for a good finger hold. Better holds lead strenuously into a groove and then on to reach the belay of the previous route.

ENGRASA LA BISAGRA MACARRA * 6c+ (E3 6b) 50ft
The third bolt line is followed on excellent holds to the base of a tiny shallow corner. The ascent of this is highly technical whether laybacking or face climbing techniques are employed. Clipping the bolt that protects the crux is difficult from below the move and easy from above it, the choice is yours. From better holds in the break swing left to an easy finish and a two-bolt belay.

T'AS PODRIO, CHAVAL ** 8a 50ft
The smooth central section of the wall just to the right is climbed with escalating difficulty until below a curious shallow depression. Entering this is best effected from the right and is desperate, leaving it to reach the belay bolts is no easier. A tough cookie.

The wall further to the right has two steep and worthwhile pitches. The first one starts just left of a thin diagonal crack.

CHICUELITO QUERIDO * 6b+ (E3 5c) 50ft
The wall is climbed on good holds past three spaced bolts to a couple of pockety moves to the belays.

ARZAPUA ** 7b 70ft
Climb the aforementioned crack to good undercuts and a breather. From here storm up the leaning wall on a miserable collection of pockets.

Further to the right is the railway tunnel and some large narrow steps that lead grippingly up to a higher level. The first route here crosses a prominent smooth grey slab from right to left.

OCEANO GRIS 7a 40ft
A technical but fairly uninspiring piece of climbing crossing the steep slab by sustained moves. Reaching the belay by doing the last few moves at a slightly higher level is technically marginally easier but somewhat more gripping.

A little further up the slope a line of bolts run up a rather scruffy looking striated wall:

PUTIFERO 5 (HVS 5a) 40ft
Follow the bolts past a small awkward roof to ledges and a single bolt lowering point. A rather better pitch than it appears from below, but then it looks pretty poor!

Right again is a fine steep grey wall bounded on the left by a smooth slab leading to a red groove. The best three pitches in this area find their respective ways up this wall.

EL VIRGO DE VISANTETA *** 6b+ (E3 5c) 100ft
Climb the steep slab past a bracketless bolt (wire hooked over it for the faint of heart) to small ledges then head up a smooth delicate scoop. Now climb up the steep groove above on excellent holds until the bolts head out onto the steep face on the right. Swing out and make a couple of fingery pulls to reach a fine sharp edged pocket. Easier climbing leads up a corner to ledges and a three-bolt belay. Abseil off.

ELTRUCO DEL ALMENDRUCO   ***   7a   100ft
A rather scruffy groove (the left-hand of two) leads to the start of the central bolt line. This gives fine sustained climbing on spaced pockets and good layaways, generally keeping to the left of the bolt ladder. Either lower off the bolt with the "tat" on it (25 metres to the ground) or continue easily to ledges and the three-bolt belay and then abseil off.

SUFRE, MAMON   ***   7a+   100ft
The right-hand line again has an uncharacteristically scruffy start but soon improves to give sustained fierce fingery climbing with the crux passing bulges at two-thirds height. Either lower off the bolt with the "tat" or safer, continue to ledges and abseil from the three-bolt belay.

The final route described is the one mentioned in the introduction as the first fully bolted route on the large walls of the areas known as FRONTALES.

To reach it walk up rightwards below the routes described above then scramble up a band of easy rock to reach a grassy bay under the cliff. Up to the right at the highest point of this an easy ramp runs up to the left. Scramble up this until it rounds a corner then put the rope on, ten minutes from the car.

EL AMPTRAX   ***   E1   560ft
A great route and a significant pointer to what these cliffs have to offer. There is no fixed gear on the first and last pitches. They are quite straightforward but it may be worth carrying a few wires "just in case".

1.   70ft   4   (Severe).   Climb easily up leftwards then follow steeper but reasonable rock to twin bolts and an old yellow peg in a niche.

2.   80ft   5   (5a).   Climb up to the left then trend back right to the foot of a smooth wall. Cross this leftwards then continue up until a couple of awkward moves can be made to the right to gain a ramp. Up this and the wall above to a five-bolt belay.

3.   70ft   5+   (5a).   Continue straight up the wall by sustained climbing to a belay at the foot of a ramp.

Colin Binks on EL AMPTRAX 5+ (E1 5b), Frontales

4.   70ft   5   (5a).   Climb up the groove on the left until it is possible to get onto the smooth looking yellow wall above and right of the stance. This is climbed on surprising holds until it eases then continue up rougher grey rock to a stance where the angle eases.

5.   90ft   5   (5b).   Climb straight up over an intimidating series of bulges until the angle drops back and easier climbing leads right and then back left to a belay below an impressive series of overhangs, fortunately the route skirts these.

6.   80ft   4   (5a).   Traverse horizontally to the right passing discrete bolts and pegs to a small stance.

7.   110ft   3+   (4b).   Climb straight up for thirty feet to an insitu thread then traverse right rising slightly (beware loose rock) to find a bright yellow cable, triple-bolt belay and mansized ring. Make three long (c.140ft) abseils from here back to the ground. On the second of these head slightly left (looking out) to locate the next anchors.

NOTE: It is also possible to abseil back down the line of the route from the top of Pitch 5 using the large rings on each stance. This avoids the rather scrappy last pitch but may prove awkward if there are other teams on the route.

Much further up the hillside is a series of impressive red caves. The largest of these is the site of a true super route, its position being identified by the fact that it crosses the most spectacular piece of rock in the area; the belay seats have been left in place!

POEMA ROCA   6c, 7c, 7b, 8a, 7a, 6c+
That should keep most people occupied for a week!

Even further up the hill is a superb and vast crack ridden slab, rising above an old quarry. It appears to be undeveloped, but then again it must be a good twenty minutes uphill walk from the track.

The only other route in the Albercones area is found by walking west towards the tunnel then just short of it cutting through a small "col" onto the open hillside. Traversing west for another 100 metres or so there is a bowl of rock. Towards the left side of this a slab leads up into a bay. This is the start of:

INSTINTO * 6a (E1 5b) 100ft

A poor start leads to a fine finish. Climb into the bay to the first bolt then swing left onto the rib (loose rock above). Climb the wall keeping left of the bolts until forced right into a small alcove. Swing left from here and make a couple of layback moves to the chains.

LOS VENENOS

Character

Los Venenos forms the front wall of the main massif at El Chorro. It consists of a fine and high, south-facing cliff with a hole punched straight through by the builders of the railway line. To the right of the tunnel is a large grey wall up which several longer routes weave their way. On some of these the fixed protection is a little spaced and so a selection of wires may be worth carrying.

To the left of the tunnel is a huge, smooth and plumb vertical wall known as the PASARELA DE LOS VENENOS. It is this face that the famous Walkway, El Camino del Rey (The King's Way), cuts across in a truly outrageous position. Parts of this Walkway are in poor condition and it is not a place for the faint of heart, though with a steady approach and a head for heights the trip through the gorge along the Walkway is a truly memorable one, (see Introduction). The routes from the Walkway tend to be steep, fingery and well protected face climbs, just the job for climbing wall buffs. Around the corner actually in the gorge, but before the Pipe Bridge is reached, are a selection of longer routes, some of which follow fine crack lines and others crossing impressive overhangs.

Access

From the parking area at ALBERCONES walk west through the first tunnel then over a high bridge and into a second tunnel. On emerging from this LOS VENENOS is dead ahead: impressive or what, definitely time for a photo session! Cross the narrow iron bridge (quickly) to reach the cliff.

The routes to the right of the tunnel are described first, from left to right. Then the climbs along the Walkway are described as they are approached ie. from right to left.

Immediately to the right of the tunnel is a short projecting buttress that contains one pleasant pitch up the prominent groove. It can be used as a quick tick, or as a convenient start to the routes

40

Los Venenos and the King's Way

that lie above. For those in a rush to get to grips with greater things it is possible to scramble up ledges that start round to the right, to gain the top of the buttress.

TECHO DE PIRATES   6a   (E1 5c)   60ft
Access to the groove is gained from the left and is quite technical with slippery footholds and unhelpful handholds, though the bolts are encouragingly spaced. Once established layback past the roof and follow the easier crack (large wires required) to a ledge and two-bolt belay. Escape down to the right or do one of the routes above.

There are four routes starting from the top of the pillar above TECHO DE PIRATES, either do it first or scramble around to the right.
Traversing above the rim of the railway tunnel is the first pitch of a long route; AMAPUL c.400 feet. After the traverse it climbs a series of steep grooves becoming increasingly overgrown as height is gained. The pitch grades are Fr.5, 6a, 6a, 6a, 5+, and double ropes will be required for the descent.

GECHA EL CIELO   **   E2   390ft
Another long and rather more worthwhile route which has its share of moments. A selection of wires should be carried if you intend to do the good top pitch. If not, either traverse right from the top of Pitch 4 or abseil back down the line of the route.
1.   40ft   4+   (4b).   From the top of the pillar trend left up easy rock with a couple of awkward moves past a solitary bolt to a good ledge with a large tree on it.
2.   60ft   6a   (5c).   Move left and gain the hanging corner with difficulty (and strenuous use of the tree branch if needed). Swing left then follow the corner, easing gradually, to a good ledge.
3.   60ft   5   (5a).   Traverse right to the end of the ledge and then climb straight up passing spaced bolts before trending right to reach a small stance with paired 'eco-bolts'.
4.   80ft   5+   (5a).   Move right to climb crack in the rib above the belay to ledges, then continue up a shallow groove moving left to a large ledge with a belay good enough to hold a train.
5.   150ft   5+   (5b).   Move up left to blocks then climb the

wall rightwards to an overhang and cross it by a bolt and a couple of archaic pegs. Climb straight up for a short distance then trend diagonally left across the fine steep slab to a large peg on the far arête. From here climb up and right to the crest of the wall. Belay ten feet higher.

Descent
From the top of the route either:

Traverse awkwardly right for twenty feet to a substantial tree and abseil down the line of the route.

or: scramble up and right then follow a steep rake down to the right with care.

YA NO ERES LO QUE ERAS   E3   100ft
A short but technical slab is the highlight of this route.
1.   40ft   4+   (4b).   From the two-bolt belay on the pillar climb up and left to a belay behind a substantial tree (as for the previous route).
2.   60ft   6b+   (6a).   Climb strenuously over the bulge and then continue up the centre of the fine but short-lived slab with thin moves at one-third height then easing to ledges and lowering bolts. It is possible to continue in the same line for another three pitches of 5 (5a), 5+ (5a), 5+ (5b) by following the previous route.

OCTOPUS DEY   ***   E4   220ft
A good climb with a couple of cracking pitches that offer fine face climbing on the right side of vertical.

Start at the two-bolt belay on top of the pillar.
1.   80ft   6c   (6a).   Move right then climb the slabby wall with escalating difficulty to pass a square roof. Above this a thin crack requires some fierce laybacking moves then swing left, (or continue direct 6b?) to the arête and continue to a good stance.
2.   60ft   6a   (5b).   Move left and climb the short wall to ledges (peg on the right), then continue up the steepening slab above to another good stance with bolt belays.
3.   80ft   6c   (6a).   Step out onto the slab on the right and mantelshelf onto a "stuck on" flake. Follow the hairline crack up the slab with sustained difficulty to reach ledges. A little higher is a bolt

belay backed up with a substantial iron bar. Make two or three abseils back to the ground.

The next route starts to the right of OCTOPUS DEY and shares its middle pitch. The start is reached by scrambling up the bank rightwards from the base of the wall to where the bushes end. A horizontal ledge leads out leftwards and is followed until it is possible to scramble up and left carefully to a ledge with a cluster of bolts.

AVION ROQUERO *** E1 210ft
Great climbing, well protected and on excellent rock.
1. 70ft   5   (5a).   Step awkwardly up and left to gain a flake and follow it to the base of a widening crack. Climb this to a bolt on a ledge, then traverse left to a belay.
2. 60ft   5+   (5b).   Step left and climb the wall and arête to ledges (peg on the right) then follow steeper rock to a good stance.
3. 90ft   5+   (5b).   Climb precariously up to an overlap (discrete peg runner) then trend right and back left before climbing straight up the slab to good belays. Descend by two abseils.

Up the bank some distance to the right are three one-pitch routes on good rock. The first two start from a four-bolt belay at the foot of a shallow but prominent left-facing corner which is reached by an arduous scramble up right and then traversing back left along ledges past a peg runner!

EMPOTRADOR 5+ (E1 5b) 70ft
From the foot of the corner climb cleaned cracks running up the slab, passing occasional fixed pieces of kit. A selection of medium and large wires is probably a good idea. From the apex of the slab lower back to the stance and perhaps have a go at top roping the next route.

PATILLAS DE JE BE 6c+ (E4 6b) 70ft
Start up the corner which is followed without incident until a line of bolts runs up the slab. These are followed with sustained technical difficulty to the tip of the slab. Lower off.

Further to the left along the ledge from the previous two routes is a short line of bolts followed by VICTIMA DE LA EVIDENCE 6a (E2 5c) 50ft, worth doing if you have made the effort of the approach to the other routes in the area.

Pasarela de los Venenos

This is the cliff above and below the Walkway. As mentioned earlier the routes are described as they are approached along the Walkway. Many of the climbs have their names painted at the base of the route to aid identification.

The first climb reached from the tunnel mouth gains a fine groove by a highly technical (and very safe) wall.

NO SEAS PESADA NENA ** (E2 6b) 60ft
Mantelshelf onto a thin ledge to clip the first bolt then make one desperate move to reach poor pockets which allow a swing right into the main groove. This gives excellent climbing sustained at about 5b until it is possible to swing left and make one last tricky move to reach the chains. Lower off.

DEMOCRATA Y CRISTIANO ** 7b 60ft
The shallow right-facing and leaning corner gives a fine sustained pitch. Gain the corner awkwardly and follow it past bolts and a thread using a variety of poor finger pockets and indifferent jams. The occasional good foothold on the right wall would ease things a lot, sadly such luxuries are few and far between.

PEDORROS MOCACACOS ** 7c+ 70ft
The next line to the left tackles a "blank" wall, one of several in this area. All that is required is fingers of steel, a touch of technical brilliance and a following wind.

To the left a pair of bolts allow access to two recent and desperate looking pitches below the Walkway. No information on grades is available but they certainly aren't V.Diff.

LES CUTRES * 6a+ (E3 6a) 50ft

Left again is an "easy" break where the rock is rather more bubbly. A leftward rising series of small ramps is reached using a variety of tiny spiky fingerholds. Traverse up and left then where the footholds run out make a couple of powerful moves to gain jugs. One more heave is required to reach the chains.

Below the previous route is a good wall climb. It is reached by abseiling from the first bolt runner on the previous route, or from the rather wobbly railing of the Walkway, to a two-bolt stance below bulges. Top roping the route lacks commitment but perhaps makes more sense!

LA CULPA LA TIENE ** 7a 60ft

Cross the bulge on layaways then easier climbing reaches a smaller bulge that is passed awkwardly to a resting place. The final wall proves to be the crux of the route and is followed by a wild swing out and mantelshelf back to the relative safety of the Walkway.

Just to the left is another "blank" wall scaled Spiderman fashion by:

JAQUE EL REY ** 7c+ 60ft

More steep face climbing on the tiniest of holds leads up and right to the finish of the previous route.

The final climb above this section of the Walkway follows a series of tiny left-trending ramps to a prominent roof.

AIXA MATINAE ** 7c+ 70ft

Scratch up the ramps by a series of precarious moves to reach the roof. Pull over this and levitate to the chains. The best way to do the final moves is to throw caution to the wind and to jump!

At the end of and below this first section of the Walkway are twin ring bolts that allow access to:

LUZ VERDE * 7a+ 70ft

Climb back up the wall and square-cut arête with sustained interest.

The Walkway now turns a corner into the gorge and rises up a series of steps. Just before a deep corner system there is a line of bolts running up an innocuous-looking grey wall on the right. This is:

MOCOS DE HIERRO * 6b (E3 6a) 50ft
The lower section of the pitch is harder than it looks and subtle use of undercuts is needed to reach a thin break and then better holds. Above this the interest is well maintained all the way to the twin bolts and the lowering chains.

The left wall of the deep corner has two fine crack lines and to their right a totally impossible looking wall climb, obviously a job for the human fly, JABEGA 8b+.

The right-hand of the pair of cracks is:

DESEOS DE DOMINIO ** 7a 80ft
A great pitch up the striking crack line, it can be converted into a three-star trip by continuing up SANTIMONIA. A thin start leads to ledges before more tough climbing is required to reach and pass the prominent roof. Move right then back left to gain a groove then an easier section leads to a good ledge. Lower off or go for the T.S.T. (Triple Star Tick).

SANTIMONIA *** E4 200ft
Another superb route.
1. 80ft 6c+ (6a). Climb the left-hand crack system by sustained laybacking and jamming until below a small overlap. From here it is possible and desirable to swing left to reach the arête. Continue up this and the crack on the right to a small stance.
2. 50ft 5+ (5b). The crack on the left gives rather more straightforward climbing to a small stance and twin-bolt belay illogically situated just below a large ledge.
3. 70ft 6b+ (6a). The third crack provides the icing on the cake offering sustained strenuous finger jamming and a dearth of footholds. From the belays make two abseils back to the Walkway.

Around the corner to the left is a magnificent towering wall tackled by a brilliant but arduous route. There is a prominent pair of bolts at thirty feet.

LA TREGVA DEL PEDAL *** 130ft

The relatively trivial first pitch can be avoided by the direct ascent of rather scruffy rock.

1.   40ft   6b+   (5c).   Slant up and right to reach the paired bolts and a restricted stance.

2.   90ft   7c+.   Follow the bolt line up the crack then continue up the wall with gradually escalating difficulty until a final desperate sequence reaches lowering chains. A sensational effort. The final steepening can be avoided by following the crack out to the arête - you wouldn't, would you?

Around the next corner along the Walkway is a series of impressive sloping roofs breached by two routes.

POLVO DE ANGLE *** 8b 70ft

The roof is taken at its widest point by an audacious piece of climbing. With good jugs the overhang would be hard enough, with the paltry set of holds supplied by Mother Nature it is one of the toughest. A lowering station is available just around the lip for the talented or jammy.

BENDERO CUMINOSO ** 6c (E4 6a) 70ft

The jamming crack through the left side of the roof provides a more reasonable trip into upside town land, at least when compared to Big Brother on the right, though make no mistakes this is no Sloth. Taping up might be a good idea if you value the back of your hands.

The next routes described are on the other side of the Pipe Bridge on the impressive cliff of CERRO CRISTO. To reach this it is necessary to cross a gap where a section of the Walkway has been removed by rock fall. A piece of railway line spans the ten-foot gap and a wire cable is available to clip into providing that you are wearing your harness. Crossing the gap without clipping in is easy for the heroic, always assuming of course that you do not slip!

*Sherri Davy crossing 'the naughty bit' on the King's Way,
the fixed grin is 'de rigeur'*

CERRO CRISTO

Character

The vast buttress (almost a mountain) on the other side of the Pipe
Bridge from the railway has a large selection of routes including
many test pieces, in a variety of settings. Most of the rock here faces
"northish" and this fact, allied with the eternal wind that blows
through the gorge means that the place is not an ideal winter venue,
though one or two of the bays are well sheltered. In summer there
are plenty of places to get away from the scorching sun. The
majority of the climbs are half rope length pitches above or below
the Walkway, though there are some longer routes thrown in for
good measure.

Access

As mentioned above most of the routes are reached from the
Walkway. From the parking place at Albercones walk along the
railway track, passing through two tunnels to reach the impressive
wall of Los Venenos. Follow the exposed Walkway around into the
gorge to reach the Pipe Bridge, taking appropriate care with "the
gripping bit". The routes are described from here as they are met
when continuing northwards around the Walkway. All this section
of the Walkway is safe enough though a modicum of care is
required as large sections have no handrail and a fall from it would
definitely prove fatal.

The first route starts from the sandy beach (La Playa) that runs
along the foot of the steep south-facing wall on the far side of the
river running through the gorge. This is reached from El Chorro by
crossing the dam and turning right. Drive along the road for a
kilometre or so until it swings left and there is a parking space on the
right. Walk back to the bend and descend to the beach. Towards the
left side of the wall is a superb left-facing corner. This is:

I'M STILL WAITING *** 6c+ (E4 6a) 90ft
The corner which has recently been rebolted gives a fine technical

pitch. Bridge the lower section of the corner until a crack appears in the back. Continue by finger jamming and laybacking until it is possible to escape across the left wall to reach a set of belays and a large ring.

Returning to the Walkway, the magnificent 300-foot grey seamed wall on the other side of the Pipe Bridge is AFRICA. Like its larger namesake the cliff is a "blank on the map", there are thrills a-plenty to be had but only by the stout hearted.

The wall contains a fine looking series of climbs in a serious setting. I have only done one route on this wall (the original AFRICA) and so this is described in full, with brief details of the other routes given where known. The crag is a great place for an adventure! It is worth pointing out that if you fail on your chosen climb the only way out is to abseil into the river and to swim for it, though at least it does not contain any crocodiles. You have been warned.

Ledges at the foot of the wall are reached by a 150-foot abseil from bolt belays with a wire cable and ring in the floor of the square-cut cave to the left of the far side of the Pipe Bridge. This is reached by crawling into the tunnel where the Pipe Bridge disappears into the cliff for a short distance until a glimmer of light is visible on the left. A narrow tunnel and short climb down leads to the square-cut cave.

As the wire belay cable hangs over the edge of the ledge getting started on the abseil is a little tricky, it is then free hanging to ledges 100 feet above the water.

From the ledges it is possible to scramble up and left to bolt belays at the foot of a fine rib that forms the left side of a large leaning wall. This is the start of:

LA DAMA DEL VIENTO *** 6b+, 6b, 6c, 6c+ c.250ft
A superb looking route that appears to be fully bolted up. It climbs the rib to a ledge system then moves right to gain a fine crack line. At the top of this it moves right again into another crack that ends below the head wall. The route finishes up this.

Traversing (roped up?) along the lowest ledge from the foot of the abseil it is possible to climb round an exposed rib and across a short slab to reach a single peg belay in a diagonal crack.

The massive groove system soaring skywards on the left at this point is:

MATERIAL BELICO   4, 5+, 6a   c.300ft
The climb appears to contain little in the way of fixed gear, a must for chimney freaks.

Directly above the peg belay is the line of:

AFRICA   ***   E4   310ft
1.   80ft   6a+   (5c).   From the peg follow an easy groove to a pair of bolts and possible stance at a line of overhangs. Pull over these into a steep corner then step right onto the wall. Climb this via a fine flake crack (Rock #5 required) to ledges and twin-bolt belay.
2.   90ft   6b+   (6a).   Climb the steep awkward crack above the stance then trend left up the wall past a small bush to gain the leftmost crack splitting this section of the face. This gives superb sustained crack and face climbing until a tricky bulge is passed and a good stance is reached.
3.   80ft   5   (5a).   A selection of runners is required from here on. Continue up the deep straight crack line to trees then a belay below the head wall.
4.   60ft   6b+   (6a).   Finish up the steep crack line in the tilted head wall.

An alternative which avoids the two upper pitches and the need to carry a substantial rack is:

3a.   100ft   5   (5a).   Traverse delicately right then continue more easily until it is possible to pull up and right onto a good ledge. From the right end of this, traverse round the corner to a substantial ring from where it is possible to lower back into the square-cut cave thirty feet below.

CHIRIPITIGLAUTICOS   5+, 6a, 5+, 6b+   c.300ft
According to the local topo this route climbs the wall to the right of Africa then joins it near the top of the crag. I have been unable to identify its exact line but at the grade given and considering the terrain it crosses it should be a classic. Any takers?

LA BELLE Y LA BESTIA *** 6a+, 7a+, 7a, 7a c.300ft
This route climbs the first pitch of AFRICA then continues straight up the disappearing crack line above. After this it bears away to the right seeking out difficulties on the steep upper walls.

To the right of the wall of AFRICA above the end of the Pipe Bridge is a short buttress capped by an overhang and containing a small collection of "short but sharp" routes.

ENIMIGO PUBLICO * 7b+ 40ft
The front wall of the buttress leads to a desperate roof, plop, drop, die or fly.

JAUJA * 7a+ 50ft
The first line on the right side of the buttress starts up a crack and continues up the wall with escalating difficulty.

GRANAIANA 85 6b (E3 5c) 80ft
This line starts as for the previous route then follows a ramp to the foot of an imposing crack which gives strenuous jamming and laybacking. This pitch would be a classic on Gogarth but the lack of bolts will doubtless lead to its total neglect here. Hopeful suitors will need a substantial rack of Friends.

E POR DOQUIER * 8a+ 60ft
To the right a short wall leads to the ramp line of the previous route. From here the route heads off up the leaning wall above, only the talented need apply.

High up the steep gully to the right is an impressively sheer grey wall with a couple of the areas very hardest routes. These are THE MONSTERS FOREVER 8b+ and CANGREO 8c, don't blame me for the grades!

The next section of CERRO CRISTO to be described is:

El Recodo

This area is found by following the Walkway around the next buttress then into a narrow ravine with a small but spectacular bridge spanning a gap. From here continue out around the next corner into a much larger bay. Most of the routes are to be found on the left (north-facing) side of this.

From the Pipe Bridge a tunnel runs through the cliff to this point but it is dark and can be wet. Which route you use depends on whether your feelings of claustrophobia or agoraphobia are greatest at the time you are trying to get to these routes.

The routes above the Walkway are described first.

On the far left side of the bay are two tiny pitches starting from blocky ledges a short distance above the Walkway.

PIXCI 6b+ (E2 6a) 20ft
The left-hand line has a tough start and awkward finish.

DIXCI 6b+ (E2 6a) 20ft
The right-hand line is a little harder and a little safer, but not a great deal more worthwhile.

Further to the right are three routes that are orders of magnitude grander.

CALIGULA *** 130ft
1.   70ft   6c.   Start in a groove to the left of a smooth brown wall and climb up to pass a bulge then continue up the crisp wall to a stance in a hole with a three-bolt belay.
2.   60ft.   7b+.   The business. Sustained face climbing follows shallow cracks in the edge of the wall with considerable difficulties until a couple of final tricky moves reach easy ground and then ledges. A triple-bolt belay is to be found over to the right.

CAMPISTA *** 7b+ 90ft
To the right is a steep wall of impressively smooth rock. This route takes the left-hand line by sustained face climbing and is protected by big beefy bolts.

MUSAS INQUIENTANTES *** 8a 90ft
The right-hand bolt line is followed throughout and a description would be superfluous, obviously both tough and magnificent.

The next selection of routes in this area all lie below the Walkway, they are mostly short, on excellent if somewhat rough rock, a place to escape the sun in summer and the crowds in winter. Several of the pitches can be top roped "à la Verdon" offering good sport without too much commitment.

The first route is found close to the left arête where it is possible to climb down behind the concrete to twin ring bolts on small ledges, and then abseil eighty feet down the wall to a twin-bolt belay in a corner.

TODOS PRETENDEN SABER ** 6c+ (E4 6a) 70ft
Step out to the left then climb up the leaning wall following the insitu gear to an awkward exit onto small ledges and twin ring bolt belays.

The rest of the routes in this area lie below CALIGULA on an insignificant looking wall that proves to be more worthwhile on closer acquaintance. The rock is excellent. The large sloping ledge at the foot of them can be approached by a twenty-five-metre abseil from a single bolt (with a painted arrow by it) on the Walkway, or by an abseil from the railings further round the bay, followed by a scramble down through the "cabbages".

An escape can be made up the back right-hand corner of the bay at about Diff if you find you have bitten off more than you can chew.

KING KONG ** 6b+ (E3 6a) 60ft
The leftmost line on the wall starting at a single bolt belay. Straightforward climbing leads to bulges that are passed on good holds. Continue to a blank section then swing left into a thin crack that proves to be a bit of a pig. Move right to the belays.

EL INDIO JUMELI ** 6b (E3 6a) 60ft

The second line from the left also starts at a single bolt belay. Climb directly up to the first bolt runner with difficulty (it might be worth clipping the first bolt on the next route if you value your ankles). Continue steeply by powerful moves on pockets and layaways to gain jugs. Cruise on to the top.

EL SIX DURU ** 6a+ (E2 5c) 60ft

Start just left of the central slanting groove at the left-hand of a pair of wire threads. Climb up the wall and through the bulges on good holds. Continue with sustained moves to a large hole on the right and exit from it awkwardly using concrete covered holds.

SIX VICIUS ** 6b (E3 5c) 60ft

The rightward slanting shallow corner which is the main feature of the wall is gained via a bulge and followed with interest to a couple of difficult moves just below the top.

TUMISMO ** 7b+ 50ft

Start at the first bolt line right of the shallow leaning groove. A tricky lower section leads to poor ledges. Swing left and pass the bolts with great difficulty.

SIETE BEL PLUMERO * 7a+ 50ft

The next line to the right (the penultimate one on the wall) is a touch easier but is no push-over. Again it features a rugged lower section and a tough upper one.

MISS DEDOS * 6c+ (E4 6a) 50ft

Start below the right-hand line at a conspicuous hole. The lower wall is climbed on rough rock and good holds to a bulging section which is a touch more problematical.

In the back of the bay above the Walkway a knotted rope hangs down from a huge cave-cum-overhang with a bit of dry-stone walling in its base. At the time of writing the roof of this is a "project" of awesome proportions. If ever completed it will be a climb of international significance, with a grade rumoured of at least 8c+.

The last routes described on CERRO CRISTO are to be found on and around the final promontory. The first route is below the Walkway as the first corner is rounded. Twin belay bolts offer access to:

LUVIA TONAL ** 5 (HVS 5a) 80ft

From a twin-bolt belay at the base of the corner follow the steep crack by bridging up into the fine sustained groove.

Continue up this on great rock until it is possible to quit it on the left to regain the Walkway. An amenable route in an impressive setting.

Around the corner (don't look down) is a niche with an impressive left wall. The first route on this is:

BOB MARLEY *** 7b+ 80ft

The bolt ladder up the leaning wall gives a great pitch on a series of generally unhelpful holds, and with escalating difficulty.

To the right, nearer the steep groove, is an even more impressive pitch up a leaning wall and over a roof, no details known, though it may be LOS CAPITALISTAS 7c. Finally on the other side of the bay there is a fine looking pitch below the Walkway. This is EXAMEN FINAL, but again no details of its grade are available, fancy an epic?

ZEPPELIN

The towering buttress that is pierced by the final tunnel on the way to Los Cotos is home to several worthwhile routes. One is long and majestic, whilst the others are short and tough. For access see the introduction to Los Cotos but stop before the last of the "three short tunnels".

Just before entering the tunnel a skeletal walkway runs out to the left above a big drop. A 130-foot abseil from the single bolt at the start of this (or the much more substantial iron loop just to the right) leads rightwards, looking out, down a fine wall to a ledge and twin-bolt belay by a tree. This is the start of a fine climb, Verdonesque in setting and rock quality. If you fail on the route a 100-foot abseil will take you down to the river from where escape is possible, either up the bank to the right of the route to the railway bridge or by wading the shallows upstream to reach the meadows below Los Cotos.

LACTARIUS DELCIOSUS ** 6b+ (E4 6a) 120ft
Step right and climb the bulge with difficulty to gain the base of the smooth wall. Continue by sustained climbing up the centre of the wall to reach good holds in the base of a crack. Step right and continue with a gradual easing in the situation eventually to gain a belay ring. Scramble off to the right. Either the Spanish grade is a bit of a sandbag, or I was having an off-day!

The other routes in this area start down by the riverside. From before the final tunnel on the way to Los Cotos follow a rather elderly walkway round to the back of the bay then descend the steep loose slope to below the railway bridge. Make an awkward descent through the left-hand arch using the preplaced railway sleeper and insitu electric flex (or abseil from the handrails on the bridge) and scramble down to the river. The base of the wall upstream from your arrival point is undercut on the right and leaning on the left. This steep piece of rock is home to three test pieces, perhaps a place for the Malham "ledge lizards" to do a bit of training before heading off home.

ZEPPELIN AREA

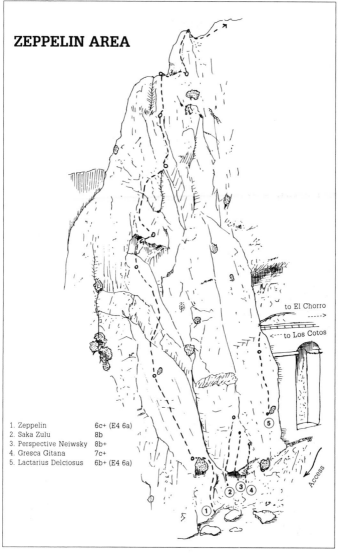

to El Chorro

to Los Cotos

1. Zeppelin   6c+ (E4 6a)
2. Saka Zulu   8b
3. Perspective Neiwsky 8b+
4. Gresca Gitana   7c+
5. Lactarius Delciosus 6b+ (E4 6a)

Access

GRESCA GITANA * 7c+ 50ft

The right-hand route tackles the large roof by a series of inventive moves. The wall above the lip is much easier.

PERSPECTIVA NEIWSKY ** 8b+ 70ft

Tackle the roof on the left where it is smaller then continue up the "radical" leaning arête above to chains just over the lip.

SAKA ZULU ** 8b 80ft

The tilted wall on the left side of this section gives a highly technical pitch that also requires considerable stamina.

ZEPPELIN *** E4 1,100ft

A magnificent expedition, the longest route in the area and a must for any competent party. The route is fully equipped with bolt runners (must have cost someone a packet) except for Pitch 6 where a small selection of wires may be of use to supplement the rather spaced insitu gear. The amount of fixed kit means that the climb can be done with a bit of "jiggery pokery" if you find you have bitten off more than you can chew. Retreat from above Pitch 4 would be awkward though not impossible, unless you are using a single rope when it would become distinctly problematical.

The start of the route is a short distance upstream of the base of the descent at a boulder beach and twenty feet left of the major corner system running up the face.

1. 90ft 4 (4b). Follow the slab into a groove. From the top of this traverse left past a peg to a bolt belay behind a large tree at the foot of the fine grey sheet of rock.

2. 120ft 6a+ (5c). Climb the centre of the big slab on good rock passing bolts, pegs and threads to a bulge which is crossed on sharp pockets. Continue until a small ledge with belays is reached.

3. 90ft 5 (5a). Tread slightly right up crack systems then follow a slanting groove up steeper rock to gain another slab. Climb this right then trend back left to a three-bolt stance below the sinister roof. This is your last chance to dip out without a mini-epic.

4. 60ft 6c (6a). A pitch done fast and free, or ambling and on aid. Climb awkwardly up to the roof then take a deep breath and head out rightwards into space. Jugs, jams and a difficult move

round a blind corner leads to a powerful pull to gain the dubious sanctuary of a wild stance. There is plenty of fixed gear on this pitch but can you stop to clip it?

5.   80ft   6c+   (6a).   Compared to the downward view this looks like a slab, don't be fooled! Swing left onto the wall where long reaches and strenuous moves between mostly (but not all) good holds gain a resting place. Move up then precariously right on shelving rock to a better ledge and belays around the corner. It is worth pointing out that a second coming adrift on this pitch could end in deep trouble.

6.   100ft   5   (5a).   Traverse right fifteen feet then follow the rather sporadic fixed gear running rightwards up the fine and surprisingly awkward slab until a final steepening leads to an uncomfortable stance on an arête below a leaning wall.

7.   90ft   6b+   (5c).   The sting in the tail. Climb the steep wall using a crack and groove until a wild swing right gains huge holds. Move up delicately to gain the steep wall and climb it strenuously on "knobblies" to a stance on the crest of the ridge.

8.   130ft   3 (V.Diff).   Scramble along the ridge and traverse up and right to pass a tower blocking the way and so reach a belay behind a tree at the foot of a corner.

9.   120ft   6b   (5b).   Climb the corner behind the belay to gain the top of the subsidiary tower. Continue up the superbly situated wall above with difficult moves at half-height and a final steepening to a belay on the crest of the ridge.

10.   220ft   4 (Severe).   Scramble along the left side of the ridge, passing behind a large flake to the base of a slab. Up this, delicately at first and then easing to gain the summit of the ridge, hoping that the resident vultures are not at home.

Descent
Follow a grassy ramp down to the left until a vague goat track can be picked up. This leads down through lycra-shredding scrub and past a very welcome watering hole, to the railway line. Twenty minutes in tight rock shoes, markedly less in trainers.

LOS COTOS

Character

Los Cotos is the most popular cliff in this guidebook and not without good reason. It is a favourite haunt of the locals and is almost invariably the initial destination of first-time visitors to the area, indeed some never stray any further. The cliff is basically a 150-foot high slab of perfect grey limestone that runs diagonally up the hillside as a continuous line of rock over half a kilometre in length. Although the upper reaches of this slab can be rather scruffy with scrub and ledges running into easier angled hillside, the lower section is a delight to climb on, perfect rock, set at a sane angle and with good protection. There are over sixty worthwhile routes here, enough to keep most people happy for a day or two!

The railway line that punches a hole through the lower section of the cliff provides easy and convenient access from the station or the parking at Albercones. The whole cliff faces due south and there is a fine selection of routes across a broad range of grades, with representatives from only the very easiest and very hardest categories missing. The rock varies between 50° and 80° in angle and so balance climbing is normally the name of the game. The majority of the pitches are well protected by bolt runners though a small selection of larger wires would not go amiss on a few of the lower grade climbs. I have indicated in the text wherever this happens to be the case.

In winter a cold wind often blows through the gorge (and roars through the railway tunnels), but the recessed situation and the aspect of Los Cotos means that if the sun is out it is almost invariably shirts off at the foot of the cliff. From the railway track the upper section of the cliff is foreshortened and looks rather insignificant. This is something of an optical illusion and these upper walls are well worth visiting especially if the lower sections are busy. There are one or two rather steeper pitches up here as well as the usual selection of climbs that require a touch of delicacy.

For any members of the team who don't want to climb, the foot of the crag is a great place for beefing up the sun tan, and with a pair of binoculars there is some fine "birding" to be had, with vultures guaranteed and a chance of plenty of other exotic species.

Access

From the parking area opposite the ALBERCONES area walk west through the first railway tunnel. Cross a high bridge and go through a second tunnel to emerge in front of the impressive cliff of LOS VENENOS with its spectacular Walkway running out above a big drop. Three more short tunnels are traversed to a long right-hand bend (beware of approaching trains which have a habit of sneaking up on you) and the cliff is found lurking just around the corner. Fifteen minutes walk from the car, twenty-five minutes from the station.

Los Cotos is split into three sections. Below the railway line and running down to the river is the COTOS BAJAS (Lower Cotos). Immediately above the railway line is the COTOS MEDIOS (Central Cotos), whilst further up the hillside stretches the COTOS ALTOS (Upper Cotos) which eventually disappears into the bank. For convenience these three sections are described separately, and in all cases the routes are described from left to right.

Cotos Bajas

A small collection of pleasant pitches down by the riverside. The waters of the Guadalhorce provide bathing or paddling but are not really to be recommended for drinking. At the right time of the year the trees on the other side of the river are heavy with oranges, providing strongly recommended free refreshments all round.

From the railway line the cliff is most easily reached by either:
1.   Following an indistinct track that branches down left about 100 yards before the tunnel cutting through Los Cotos, care required towards the bottom where the slopes are rather unstable, or:
2.   By heading right to the foot of the COTOS MEDIOS and walking through the steep drainage tunnel that runs beneath the railway line.

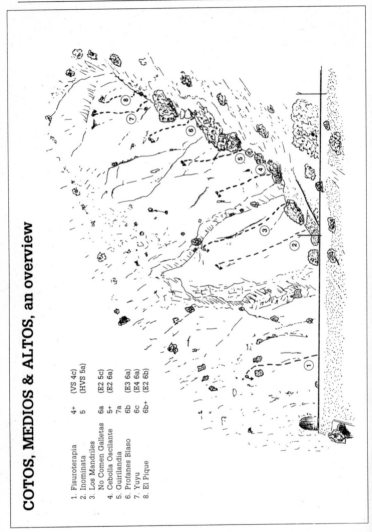

COTOS, MEDIOS & ALTOS, an overview

1. Fisuroterapia   4+   (VS 4c)
2. Inominata   5   (HVS 5a)
3. Los Mandriles
   No Comen Galletas   6a   (E2 5c)
4. Cebolla Oscilante   5+   (E2 6a)
5. Gurilandia   7a
6. Profanes Biaso   6b   (E3 6a)
7. Yuyu   6c   (E4 6a)
8. El Pique   6b+   (E2 6b)

Mike Appleton and Nig Baker on Pitch 2 of
PILLIER DORADA 6c (E4 6a), El Polverin

It is also possible to approach the Cotos Bajas from the Upper Gorge and El Polverin which lies just through the next tunnel, but this requires care as the rocky slope that runs from the base of El Polverin down to Los Cotos is steep and awkward.

At the very left-hand edge of the cliff is a short, grey, triangular slab of good rock containing two minor routes. The left line is:

ORINADA SALVAJE 5+ (E1 5c) 40ft
Climb easily to the first bolt and pass it leftwards with considerable difficulty, especially considering its Spanish grade. Better holds lead to a bulge and a solitary and rather wobbly belay bolt, lower off carefully.

MAMA QUIERO SER TORERO 6a (E3 6a) 40ft
Follow the right-hand line past a dicky bolt to a better one just a little higher. Sketchy moves on very thin holds and a random collection of pathetic pockets lead with difficulty to deeper pockets, and a third bolt. From here a traverse left leads to the wobbly bolt belay of the previous route. Lower off gently. Another route that throws a spanner in the works of comparative grading systems.

To the right are some evergreen bushes and just beyond these a thin crack with a small but conspicuous finger pocket a short distance up its left side. This crack is the start of:

SAN SATANAS *** E2 5c (6a) 100ft
A fine pitch following an elegant curving line up the wall above the bushes. The bolts are rather spaced so it is probably worth taking a small selection of mid-range wires to supplement them.

Climb the crack awkwardly (Rock 5) to deep flaky jugs and the first bolt. Move up then traverse delicately left to eventually reach a prominent rock scar. From here continue straight up by sustained climbing to reach bolt belays. Abseil off.

Chris Craggs enjoying a bit of Christmas spirit on
ZOMBI COMBI 6a+ (E2 5c), El Torcal

SAN GABRIEL ** HVS 110ft

Start at the name painted on the rock below a discontinuous line of flakes and pockets. Take a standard rack for the first pitch as it contains no fixed gear.

1. 60ft 4 (4c). Follow the flake system using a set of fine but well spaced holds. These gradually bear away to the left to reach a collection of bolts that provide the belays in a rather cramped recess.

2. 50ft 4+ (5a). Climb straight up from the belay over a series of bulges following the line of bolts to reach the very substantial belays. Either belay here then abseil off or lower back to the first stance and abseil from there.

LA HORA DEL MAQUIS * 5+ (E1 5b) 80ft

Start at a thin crack containing a very insubstantial looking thread runner at fifteen feet. Take a few mid-range and large wires.

Climb the crack to reach the first bolt ensuring that you don't fall off before you clip it, as if the thread did not break the rock it is around probably would! Continue with sustained interest into a shallow corner then either climb up leftwards (wires) to belays in a hollow, or bear right to the belays of the next route. Many parties lower off from the last bolt runner which is fine as long as the bolt is a good one!

LA PLACA MORROCOTUDA *** 6a (E2 5c) 90ft

A fine varied pitch up the front of the narrow buttress to the right buttress. Take a few large wires. Start from the tip of a fallen flake and climb the edge of the wall before stepping left and continuing straight up to bulges. Continue up the crack (large wires) then bear right up flakes until it is possible to step back left onto some small ledges. A thin move up and right to past a bolt provides the crux of the pitch after which there remains a romp to the belay. Lower off.

To the right just before the bushes close in completely is a fine, clean rib with a closely spaced line of bolts running up it. This is:

BERRINCHE DE CHINCHE ** 6b (E3 6a) 60ft

A great little pitch sustained and safe. The crux is at two-thirds height where a stuck-on flake has to be used to make strenuous moves to gain a "surprising" ledge. Easier climbing leads to the belay.

The wall running away towards the railway line contains a couple of scruffy pitches that are not really worthy of attention unless you have done everything else in the area.

The first is a cleaned crack twenty metres right of the last route. This is EL YERNO DE ABRAHAM 50ft 6a and it requires a rack of nuts, thus ensuring its continued obscurity.

Further to the right and just before the tunnel is a wall with three spaced bolts. This is CUATRO MEJILLONES ZO DUROS 40ft 6c+. Lower off the last bolt.

The smooth scooped wall immediately to the left of the railway tunnel has a short but desperate looking pitch starting from a flat ledge which is reached by an awkward scramble. No details are known but it should provide sport for those fortunate enough to be "strong of finger and light of build".

Cotos Medios

The slabby section of rock immediately above the railway line is a very popular area for climbing, sunbathing or just taking the air. It contains a good selection of bolt-protected routes, many of which are at an amenable angle and in the lower grades, a rare combination indeed. Access from the railway is obvious. The first routes described lie just above the tunnel that runs underneath the railway line.

CAMELLO COJO ** 5 (HVS 5a) 90ft
This climb starts from twenty feet up the gutter at the left end of the cliff. Carry a standard rack. The crack running slightly rightwards up the steep slab gives a pleasantly sustained pitch and even contains a solitary bolt. At the top trend right to big bolt belays behind a tree. Abseil off.

FISUROTERAPIA *** 4+ (VS 4c) 90ft
A great pitch, sustained and interesting.

Start six feet right of the edge of the wall and follow the sustained crack line running straight up the steepening slab. Holds are generally good and the route contains a smattering of bolts, carry a selection of wires (especially Rock 9s galore) to plug the gaps unless you are feeling particularly heroic. Belay behind the tree as for the previous route.

FISORA DE LOS SANTOS *** 5 (VS 4c) 100ft
Another cracking pitch. Start as for the previous route. Carry a few large wires. Follow the crack for a short distance then bear right to below the left-hand of a pair of wide bulging cracks splitting the steepest part of the slab. This is climbed on great holds to reach more amenable rock above. Climb this direct or more easily rightwards to reach a solitary bolt. Traverse left to reach the belay of the previous two routes and abseil off.

FISORA DE HAMBRE *** 5 (HVS 5a) 110ft
The third and best of a great trio, the kind of route you have been hungering for, the bolts in it being both large and frequent. Climb directly up the slippery and unprotected slab to the first bolt in the right-most line or gain it more safely from the previous routes. Continue up and right to reach and ascend the wide right-hand crack by sustained and interesting climbing. Continue rightwards up a pleasant slab to substantial belays. Abseil off.

To the right is an easy break and then fifteen metres up the slope a short, clean slab with bushes at its foot and an undercut left corner. It contains three short routes.

BITCHITOS ON THE WAILERS * 4+ (HVS 5a) 50ft
A route worth doing if only for the name. Climb awkwardly over the overhang at the foot of the wall. This is distinctly problematical unless you use a good but unobvious layaway on the left. Continue up the pleasantly sustained slab to lowering bolts.

EL MONSTRUO DE LAS GALLETAS 5+ (E1 5b) 70ft
Start just to the left of the bushes and climb up and right (machete required to get started) to the left-hand pair of bolts in the centre of

Mike Bartley on FISUROTERAPIA 4+ (VS 4c), Los Cotos

the slab. A short sustained section past these leads to easier climbing and then ledges. Above these are some discrete wire threads to belay on. It is probably best for the last man to abseil off these to avoid damaging the rope.

MORDISCOS DE AMOOR 5 (HVS 5a) 70ft
Start to the right of the bushes and slant up and left to reach and follow the right-hand line to the same discrete belay of the previous climb. The comments about getting back down apply to this route as well.

To the right is another easy gully/break and then a large, clean, triangular slab bounded by a scruffy corner on the right and with a series of ledges just below its apex. This slab is always popular because of its accessibility and also because of the quality and grade of the routes on it. Most people start their El Chorro apprenticeship here.

ALUCINOS ** 4 (VS 4c) 70ft
The left-hand line on the slab is a thin crack starting a short distance up the cliff. To further aid identification the second bolt is a blue one. A tricky start gains the first bolt and a little higher is a resting ledge. Continue with interest to the final bolt which is passed rightwards using poor slippery holds (crux) to reach easy ground. A three-bolt belay lies up to the right, thread and lower off from the ring bolt but clip the others if you are top roping people up the pitch.

INOMINATA *** 5 (HVS 5a) 70ft
The second line of bolts starts one metre left of the edge of the paving and gives an excellent sustained piece of climbing on small holds and with exemplary protection, a real clip up. Enjoy it while you can as there is absolutely nothing like it back home, then lower off.

To the right is a bush and just left of this a crack line runs diagonally rightwards up the slab starting from the edge of the paving. This is:

NUMBER 1 *** 4 (VS 5a) 80ft
The bolt-protected crack is followed with interest to its end where thinner moves are made back left past two more bolts to reach the belays, lower off.

BRUJA INTREPIDO ** 5 (HVS 5a) 80ft
Between the two left-hand sets of bushes is a line of bolts rising slightly leftwards up the slab. These are followed by sustained moves until the previous route is joined, finish up this and lower off from its belays.

NUMERO DOS * 5 (HVS 5a) 90ft
To the right of the second patch of bushes is yet another line of bolts running straight up the slab and starting from a small, flat area surrounded by greenery. The rather spaced bolts are followed throughout to join and finish up the last section of the next route. From the edge of the slab descend to the left to reach the belays above the finish of the previous routes. A pleasant but unremarkable piece of exercise when compared to its partners to the left.

GALLETA * 4 (VS 4b) 120ft
Before the slab starts to steepen up there is a diagonal break rising across it from right to left and sprouting assorted greenery. This is followed past spaced peg runners, take a selection of wires to supplement these. From where the break ends traverse left then descend diagonally to the left to reach the belays used by the previous routes. Perhaps not the kind of route for nervous seconds. Abseil off.

SUPER GALLETA *** 5+ (E1 5b) 100ft
A superb pitch that starts at the foot of the diagonal break of the previous route. The name is painted discreetly in black "echo" paint twenty-five feet up the route. Follow the line slightly leftwards up steepening rock into a shallow groove. This gives sustained climbing with the expected jug never quite materialising. From the last bolt make a couple of awkward moves then trend right up easier rock and then ledges with substantial belays. Abseil off.

71

Pete Blackburn on SUPER GALLETA, 5+ (E1 5b), Los Cotos

To the right is a steep, left-facing corner groove and to its left is a bulging wall taken by:

GABY ** 6b+ (E3 6a) 90ft

Climb straight up into the base of the steep corner then traverse left on to the face. This gives sustained climbing, small holds and the occasional blind move before eventually joining the final easy section of the previous route.

LOS MANDRILLES NO COMEN GALLETAS *** 6a (E2 5c) 90ft

Another great route with a lot of good climbing. The long corner is entered from directly below and followed awkwardly on a series of strange rugged holds to resting ledges below the steeper upper section. This is climbed with difficulty past a peg runner; small pocket holds around the right arête of the groove may be found useful until the situation eases and much more straightforward moves lead to solid belays. Abseil off.

MADRILLES ** 7a 80ft

The wall that hangs above the previous route contains some conspicuous hand-sized, rounded pockets and provides a taxing pitch. Climb easily to the second bolt and pass it with difficulty to gain the first hole. More tough moves lead left then straight up on a series of indifferent holds until the situation eases. Either lower off the last bolt in the slab or continue easily to more substantial anchors higher up and abseil off these.

To the right is the long, scruffy corner that bounds this section of cliff, doubtless it would be a well glossed classic back home but at the moment it awaits the attentions of someone of vision. Around to the right is a rather scrappy slab that is the home of a two-pitch climb: EMPOTRADOR EMOTRADO 4+ which trends left up the slab. This appears to contain no fixed gear and requires a soul with a rack of wires and a strong sense of adventure.

A little further to the right is a steep, grey slab with a prominent triple-bolt and hefty chain belay. This is:

LA CEBOLLA OSCILANTE ** 5+ (E2 6a) 70ft
The lower section of the route gives straightforward and pleasant climbing, with small holds and the odd mantelshelf manoeuvre. From the final bolt runner difficult moves are made on the left or the right with a final gripping teeter to reach the belays. If all else fails try jumping.

The slabs hereabouts offer considerable scope for new routing on quality rock at a reasonable angle. A little project perhaps when you have done all the other routes on Los Cotos.

Cotos Altos

The upper section of Los Cotos offers a fine selection of routes often with starts on strangely smooth rock. The rather featureless nature of large sections of the wall makes the identification of individual routes quite difficult on first acquaintance, especially as very few of the names of the climbs are painted on the rock. A trip up along the base of the cliff with the guidebook, identifying some of the more prominent features may turn out to be time well spent.

Access along the very foot of the rocks is rather tortuous because of bushes and boulders. Fortunately a rough path ascends the slope a short distance out from the wall, offering an easier approach and allowing a better view of the cliff. After rain, parts of this path are distinctly unstable, not a place for the wearers of slick-soled footwear.

To the right of the prominent triple-bolt and chain belay on LA CEBOLLA OSCILANTE is a section of undeveloped rock and then after twenty metres a long vegetated and ragged crack line. To the right of this is a large crystalline block on the ground with two thin cracks above it both with two bolt runners. These offer a couple of quick ticks and are:

GENESIS 5 (E2 5c) 40ft
The left-hand crack has a couple of entertaining moves before easing rapidly. Lower off.

MONGROVI FREE 6b (E2 5c) 40ft
Despite the Spanish grades the right-hand crack is perhaps a touch

more amenable and leads with a quick sprint to the same lowering point.

To the right a long thin crack runs up the slab, it has a couple of old bolt studs at the left side of its lower section. The crack is followed in part by:

ARBOLA ** 6a+ (E2 6a) 60ft
A slippery start gains the deeper section of the crack which is followed until it becomes very thin. Either continue up it with considerable difficulty to the belay or rather more easily, step right before trending back to the left to reach the anchors, lower off.

BRUNER AND THE BRUNA *** 6a+ (E2 5c) 80ft
To the right of the thin crack of ARBOLO is a conspicuous small round hole a short distance up the cliff. Climb onto a sloping ledge below and left of this starting at a broken flake, then traverse delicately to the right and step up into the hole. Move up to the second bolt then step awkwardly down and left into a hollow before moving up and right to easier rock. (The technically proficient can avoid all this weaving about and do the whole thing direct.) Continue up the bulging wall with sustained interest and one distinctly thin section to reach the belays.

LEY DE LA SELVA ** 6b+ (E3 6a) 80ft
Start at the name painted on the rock. Climb up and left clipping in to but keeping to the right of the green bolts. Better holds lead up steeper rock to a well exercised bolt in a smoother section of wall. Make a difficult mantelshelf to the left of the bolt then head up and right to pass it with great difficulty. Handholds consist of a couple of razor blades and there is a distinct lack of footholds. Above this better holds and easier climbing lead to the lowering bolts and a wire cable.

To the right is a steep, clean slab suspended above a steeper section of rock that rises across the cliff from right to left. The name GUIRILANDIA is painted at the base of the cliff. This area contains some fine pitches almost too steep to be described as slabs.

EMBOLIA CEREBRAL ** E1 120ft

A pleasant two-pitch route in which the bolts are quite spaced. There are not many cracks on the route so carrying a large rack of wires is probably a waste of time. Be bold.

1. 50ft   5+   (5b).   From just left of the name GUIRILANDIA climb a slippery slab leftwards to the first bolt. Continue up the bulging wall with interest on good but spaced holds to a twin-bolt belay where the angle eases.

2. 70ft   5   (5a).   Follow the ramp up to the left past a trio of bolts then climb straight up with continuous interest to a large but solitary belay bolt in the middle of the slab. Lower back to the stance then abseil to the ground.

THE POLICEMAN STOLE MY WALKMAN *** 6b (E3 5c) 80ft

There is doubtless an interesting story behind this route name. Start as for the previous route and follow it to the two belay bolts (5b). From here trend up and then right across the steep slab by sustained climbing on small holds with the crux being the last couple of moves to reach a prominent large bolt. It is at this point you may wish that your trusty second was not quite so far away and that the rope drag was a little less noticeable. A little higher is a ramp system with belays down to the right. Abseil off.

GUIRILANDIA *** 7a 80ft

Start at the name and climb easily to the band of steeper rock. Move left and gain the slab with difficulty and follow it on "match edges" and poor slopers. Protection is good throughout but the majority of the holds are a distinct disappointment, the pitch is a real must for "slate heads".

CAFE BONK ** 7a+ 80ft

Start to the right of GUIRILANDIA and follow a direct line up the steep wall, passing the large scratched arrow with great difficulty. Once established on the slab make horribly thin moves to safety. Most certainly not a route for your average muscle-bound gorilla.

The right side of the steep slab is bounded by a curious shallow right-facing groove, a small water-worn channel. Below this is a

CAFE BONK 7a+, Los Cotos. A must for 'slate heads'

solitary bolt in the slab, start below and left of this.

PENETRATION ANALGESIA ** 6b+ (E3 6a) 80ft
Climb on to a ledge and move right to clip the first bolt. This is passed by a thin and slippery (English 6b for the short?) move to gain ledges at the foot of the groove. This is awkward to enter and is followed with sustained difficulty, though fortunately there are more holds than is initially apparent from below. At the top of the groove move up and left to belays. Abseil off.

To the right is a short slanting crack with three bolts in the wall to its left. This is:

SI TE "CAES" PEGA UNA VOZ 6b+ (E2 6b) 30ft
The crack is short but slippery and desperate. If you can do it without at least one slither, then you can award yourself "una cerveza grande".

To the right the base of the cliff rises up in a step and a crescent-shaped ledge system cuts across the base of a heavily scarred wall. Starting below the lowest point of this crescent is:

AMARILLA ** E1 140ft
A pleasant sustained route, carry a few large wires for the second pitch.
1. 60ft   5   (5b).   Mantelshelf onto the ledge then traverse out to the left to reach the line of bolts. This is followed with continuous interest by delightful balance climbing to small ledges and bolt belays.
2. 80ft   5+   (5a).   Move left to the foot of a rather grassy looking crack which is followed on mostly good holds to a final couple of delicate moves to an old solitary bolt. Move right to find its much more substantial modern counterparts. Abseil off.

FANATICOS DEL ALICO ** 140ft 6c (E4 6b)
Follow the first pitch of AMARILLA then continue up the fine grey face directly above the stance. There is no shortage of bolts but a distinct dearth of good holds, sustained thin moves giving pleasure

*Colin Binks on the crux of GUERREROS DEL ABISMO 6c+ (E4 6b),
perhaps the best pitch on Los Cotos*

79

(or pain) a-plenty, thin with a capital "TH".

EL VENTO ** E2 160ft
1. 70ft   5a   (5).   Start to the right of where the curving ledge system reaches the ground and climb straight up to a ramp which is followed leftwards past one set of belays to those used on the previous route.
2. 90ft   5c   (6a+). Move up and right to reach a thin crack with a large square-cut scar on its left side. This is followed by sustained moves and with spaced bolts and occasional use of the crack on the right, eventually to reach a tree and large belays. A few mid-range and large wires would not go amiss to supplement the fixed gear on this pitch, quite bold.

LA BLANCA ** E3 160ft
A pleasant first pitch leads to a tougher challenge on the upper wall, where double ropes might help to reduce rope drag.
1. 60ft   5a   (5).   As for EL VENTO but belay on the first set of bolts instead of continuing the traverse.
2. 100ft   6a   (6b).   Move up to the bulge and pull through it rightwards past a bolt and then peg runners to gain easier angled rock. Climb up and right and then back left before going straight up to ledges, crux. More straightforward climbing up cracks leads to easy ground. Move left to the belays and then abseil off.

Above and to the right of the bottom end of the ramp used in part by EL VENTO is the steepest section of Los Cotos. Fortunately it is split by a fine series of thin cracks and these offer a series of challenging routes. Starting a short distance to the left of the point where the ramp reaches the ground and below a prominent small tree at forty feet is:

GUERREROS DEL ABISMO *** 100ft 6c+ (E4 6b)
Climb to the ramp then attack the soaring thin crack line above with conviction, until just below a tree. Make a technical traverse out right to a lumpy foothold then deal with the crux section. With fortitude, strong fingers and slick footwork the belay ledges are

Colin Binks nearing the top of the superb SEGOVIA 6a (E2 5c), El Torcal

eventually reached; brilliant and perhaps the best pitch on the crag. Abseil descent.

EXCESO DE EQUIPAJE ** 80ft 6b+ (E4 6a)

The next crack to the right starting from the very base of the leftward-trending ramp line gives a fine sustained pitch with much less fixed gear than the name might suggest. Carry a selection of wires unless you have got your bold head on. The crack is followed slightly rightwards by sustained moves until it eventually bears away to the right to ledges and twin lowering bolts of the previous route.

Right again and to the left of a huge conglomerate boulder on the ground is a thin crack that splits into two as it rises. The left fork is taken by:

CHUNGO SUPERIOR ** E2 150ft

1. 80ft 5+ (5b). Follow the crack using a combination of face holds and finger jamming. The bolts are well spaced so carry a selection of mid-range and large wires to supplement them.
2. 70ft 6a (5c). More of the same and still with rather too few bolts for comfort. From the top make one long or two short abseils back to the ground from the solitary bolt.

QUASIMODO ** 7a+ 80ft

The right fork gives a real battle with poor finger holds and even poorer footholds. Eventually the crack kinks back to the left and the situation eases. Lower off from the first belay of the previous route.

To the right of the thin cracks is the previously mentioned conglomerate boulder on the floor and then a pile of red blocks. Further to the right is a large boulder lying against the cliff with a prominent bolt low down in the wall to its left.

PROFANES BLASO *** 6b+ (E3 6a) 90ft

Climb past the initial bolt with difficulty and clip the second one with trepidation. Once this is done move up and right to ledges. Gain the crack above and follow it with sustained pleasure until a

---

Bill Gregory on SU DIOS EXISTE, ES SU PROBLEMA 7b, Mijas, 31st December 1990. What a way to end the year!

couple of steep and sneaky moves allow access to easier angled rock and a little higher the lowering anchors.

The next easily identifiable feature to the right is a flat wall with a curving crack line rising from right to left across it and meeting a very thin crack that cuts straight up the wall from behind a great flat block. The vertical crack is protected by two bolts and is:

PISTO GILGERO * 6c+ (E3 6b) 60ft
Short and sharp.
Climb easily to the first bolt then make a couple of decidedly sketchy moves past the second one to finger jams and then better holds. Romp on to the belay with a growing feeling of self satisfaction. Lower off or try the steep slab and roof above, (EL DINAMITA TE ESPERA, see below).

QUE TE DEN POR CULO ** E3 5c (6b) 70ft
This route follows the curving crack line that runs diagonally up the slab. It starts off amenably enough but turns into an increasingly harrowing hand traverse. When all appears lost it is necessary to mantel into the break and then continue with relief to the belay above the last route. Lower off or belay here and then have a crack at:

EL DINAMITA TE ESPERA ** E3 6a (6c) 80ft
Climb the straightforward steep slab to a possible belay then attack the centre of the impressive overhang. If successful the belays are not far away, if not then its back into the gym when you get home.
To the left of this last route is a good looking pitch up the hanging rib, though no details are available. It certainly looks easier than the roof tackled by EL DINAMITA....

YUYU *** 6c (E4 6a) or 6a (E2 6a) 120ft
A great route with contrasting styles subtly blended.
Start as for the previous route but move right to gain a curving overlap. Either follow this round to the left and make committing moves (E4) to ledges, or more easily step right and climb the rib (E2) until it is possible to move left and join the "proper" way. From the

joining of the ways either belay down on the left or much better press on. Climb up the bulging slab with interest especially at the steepest section then pad Etive like up to the belays. Descend by one long or two short abseils.

A short distance to the right is a short line of bolts running straight up a steep slab:

CHULO DE MADRIZA * 7a 40ft
The line is followed with sustained difficulty. Strong fingers and a degree of technical ability are needed to guarantee success on the first attempt.

Right again is a long crack line slanting up to the right. Unfortunately it does not quite reach the ground though a providently placed boulder on the right allows access to it.

EL PIQUE ** 6b+ (E2 6b) 90ft
A fine pitch rather spoilt by the desperate moves up and left from the block to gain the foot of the crack. If all else fails the use of one metal handhold can overcome this and the rest of the pitch provides fine sustained climbing on good holds and with a tricky little traverse round a bulge thrown in for good measure. From the final bolt trend blindly rightwards to the belay.

PETAMORPHOSIS *** 7a+ 80ft
From part way up the crack of EL PIQUE move out onto the wall and make a long series of sustained moves to reach eventually twin ring bolts where there is an easing in the angle. Lower off from these. A superb piece of climbing on spaced holds and smooth rock.

The steep smooth rock immediately to the right of the last route is reputed to be the home of an 8a climb THE BUTTER FINGER. At the time of writing there are no bolts visible in this section of rock, so perhaps the route is a hoax, whoever heard of an 8a slab anyway (well apart from on slate?).

The final section of routes is to be found up to the right where the cliff finally disappears into the hillside. The most obvious features are a ramp line running up to the left and just beyond this two left-facing corner systems. The first route here follows the ramp line and the crack above its end.

Start at the foot of the left-trending ramp:

MISTER PROPER ** E1 130ft
It might be worth carrying a few mid-range wires to supplement the bolts, though cracks are few and far between.
1. 70ft   5+   (5b).   Traverse up the ramp delicately passing spaced bolts until the climbing eases and it is possible to head straight up a thin crack line to a sloping stance.
    It might be a good idea to clip the bolt to the right of the start of this pitch in case of a slip from the first tricky moves.
2. 70ft   4+   (5a).   Continue up and right onto the steeper wall and then head back left to reach another good stance directly above the first. One long abseil or two short ones will take you back to base.

The thin crack with three bolts in it below the ramp on pitch one can be used as a rather tough (English 6a) direct start to this route or as a reasonably graded (still English 6a) indirect start to the next one.

EL VIAJERO AMABLE *** 6b+ (E3 6a) 70ft
Superb sustained face climbing with enough bolts to allow the experience to be enjoyed to the full. Follow the previous route to the first bolt and then continue up the deliciously sustained steep slab above until the angle drops back and it is possible to pad straight on up to a belay.

ADELI ** 6b+ (E2 6a) 70ft
To the right of the foot of the ramp is a thin polished crack with a bolt on its left side. Slither up the crack then step left (the second bolt is a bit of a gripper clipper) to follow the rib on a fine and surprising selection of holds. The belays are found away on the left, as for the previous route.

Right again is a curiously scalloped groove which provides an interesting and elegant pitch.

ELECTRO VOLT ** 6b+ (E1 6a) 70ft
Gain the base of the groove with difficulty (crux) then pad up it by technical bridging with plenty for the feet and very little for the hands. At the closure of the groove pull over onto easier angled rock and romp up and right to the belays.

The final feature of the wall is another groove, it is well worth the walk up.

EXODO ** E2 6a (6a+) 70ft
The groove is gained from the right and gives a pleasant pitch on slippery rock, thank goodness for sticky boots. At its top is a solitary and rather old bolt, so traverse to the left to the finish of the previous route and use its belays to lower off from.

The bolt in the steep slab to the left of the start of EXODO is the protection on a short-lived but tough direct start:

POEMA VERTICAL 7b+ 70ft
If you can get past the bolt the regular route is a path by comparison.

EL POLVERIN

Character

A superb cliff of pocketed grey limestone which is vertical or gently overhanging throughout almost all of its length. Towards its right edge the cliff is over 250 feet high but most of the best routes are concentrated towards the left side where an unbroken wall rises shear for 150 feet. In some places the routes appear to be rather close together though in fact once embarked on your chosen pitch they invariably feel quite independent enough. Several of the routes have paired ring bolt anchors just below the cliff top to allow either a "Yoyo" back to the stance or an abseil to the base of the cliff. If you top out you will find wire cables running along the cliff top leftwards following narrow exposed ledges to easy ground. It is STRONGLY recommended that you keep the rope on and clip into these cables on the way past. A slip from these sloping ledges would almost certainly give a considerable shock to any parties operating below and may dent more than your ego!

The majority of the climbs on this fine face are E3 and E4. Despite this a pleasant day's cragging can be had at a more amenable grade by doing the lower pitches of the longer routes and then lowering back to the ground from the substantial ring bolts that decorate all the stances hereabouts.

The cliff faces west and so in the winter season is best enjoyed in the afternoon sunshine though the sun actually disappears behind the high hills to the west of the gorge by about 4.00pm. In summer an early start and climbing in the cool of the morning should enable a good time for cragging whilst avoiding too much of a roasting. Except for the lower section of PACO EUGENE all that is required to climb here is a rope (or two) and a bunch of quick draws, up to 14 are needed on the biggest pitches. After climbing here High Tor will never seem quite the same again.

Access

From the parking place at ALBERCONES follow the directions to reach Los Cotos and then to reach the left side of EL POLVERIN

EL POLVERIN

1. Svenos De Venos   6a   (E2 5b)
2. Habitos De Un Pertubo
   Irremersible   6c   (E4 6a)
3. La Pregiero Tontas/
   Games Moya   6c   (E4 6a)
    4. Nirvana   6b+ (E4 6a)
    5. Los Cocodrilos
      No Lloran   7a+
6. Paco Eugene   6a   (E1 5b)
7. El Engrendo   5+   (E1 5b)
8. Jaquima   6b+ (E3 6a)

continue through the next tunnel. This is curved and from the entrance appears longer than it really is. Once through this, admire the newly revealed view and then turn left and follow a short horizontal path to a shoulder overlooking the cliff. Twenty minutes from the car park. Gear up here then cross ledges and scramble down to the left side of the face. The small building with the rounded roof sited above the path is a viable bivi shelter being both clean and dry. Please respect this and avoid using it as a toilet.

To reach the very foot of the cliff for PACO EUGENE and JAQUIMA follow the directions for COTOS BAJAS and walk around the corner at the left edge of the cliff before bashing through the bushes to reach a level area at the lowest point of EL POLVERIN.

The routes are described from left to right.

ALERTA ROJA *** 6b+ (E4 6a) 160ft

A really great route which feels rather "squeezed in" in its lower section but becomes increasingly worthwhile as height is gained. A friend told me he thought the grade was E2 5c - you decide!

Start in the steep narrow gully at the very left edge of the cliff (arrow) and climb the easy wall to the first bolt. Layback the awkward cracks just to the left then climb a short wall in the base of a shallow groove (SVENOS DE VENENOS). From here swing left onto the steep wall and climb it past a big pocket, with sustained and considerable difficulties. At the level of the stalactite swing left and climb up to a tufa pillar below the prominent tree. Traverse left around this and then finish more easily up a grey slab. Belay on the right on a massive steel ring.

SVENOS DE VENENOS *** E2 150ft

The easiest route on the main part of the face but no push-over offering steep and sustained climbing coupled with impressive situations.

1. 50ft   5   (5a).   Climb easily up into a wide crack near the left side of the face and its closure (bolt) traverse out to the right to reach juggy flakes and just a little higher a three-bolt belay.

2. 100ft   6a   (5b).   Traverse left for fifteen feet passing two well hidden peg runners to a steep shallow groove and follow it by

Chris Craggs stretched out on the crux moves on SVENOS DE VENENOS VARIATIONS 6a+ (E3 5c), El Polverin

sustained climbing on good but spaced holds and occasional good jams deep inside holes until it begins to bulge. From here trend left up the wall and across the bulges via a stalactite before jug pulling your way to glory and a belay big enough for mooring the QE2.

SVENOS DE VENENOS VARIATIONS *** 6a+ (E3 5c)

A variation start and finish to the parent route can be combined to give a great way up the cliff, well worth doing.

Start at a short right-facing flake near the left side of the face and climb directly up the wall to the second bolt runner. Step left to the top of the wide crack then cross the smooth slab on the left with difficulty to gain the base of the main groove. Up this to its top then press on up the wall to a roof with a bolt in its lip. Pull over to the left of the bolt on good holds then climb up to a discrete yellow bolt before traversing left to a belay on the big ring.

The next three routes all have the same first pitch.
Start at GENERATION EXPONTANEA painted on the rock in discrete lettering.

PILLIER DORADA *** E4 104ft

A fine second pitch offering sustained and powerful climbing up magnificent rock.
1. 50ft   6a   (5b).   As for GENERATION EXPONTANEA (see below) to the three-bolt stance.
2. 90ft   6c   (6a).   Traverse left for ten feet (low peg) then climb the crack to the right of the rib to its end. Swing left and make difficult moves to a large pocket (crux). More hard moves are required before things begin to ease a little. Good holds and thin moves alternate in a way sure to tire your arms and your mind at a steady rate until an inverted niche is reached. Finish more easily through this. A measured approach is definitely the name of the game on this pitch.

GENERATION EXPONTANEA *** E3 140ft

A great climb of escalating interest.
1. 50ft   6a   (5b).   Start at a small but prominent undercut pocket then continue directly and with interest (and also a

monodoigt) to reach good flakes and just a little higher a three-bolt belay at a series of small ledges.

2. 90ft   6b+   (6a).   Trend left up the wall following a series of large but often unhelpful pockets until the rock becomes "blank". Make a difficult finger traverse to the right to better holds then climb back left to jugs. A final steep wall has well spaced bolts and (fortuitously) good holds and is taken slightly rightwards to reach a comfy cave with a huge wire thread. Either continue easily to the top, lower back to the stance from the paired ring bolts in the left edge of the cave, or abseil from the cable.

REVUELTA EN EL OPATICO   ***   E5   140ft

1. 50ft   6a   (5b).   As for GENERATION EXPONTANEA to the small ledges and three-bolt belay.

2. 80ft   7a   (6a).   Climb straight past a large yellow bolt and on up the steepening wall until it becomes smooth. Step right and make a long pull for small fingerholds above which the situation begins to ease a little. The steep white wall is climbed keeping to the left of the bolts until it is possible to move left to reach the cave stance on GENERATION EXPONTANEA and lower off, or continue straight up to the cliff top as for the next route.

According to the local topo a right-hand start is possible to the crux pitch of the last route at about the same grade and is even graced with its own name, ALIPISMOS HISTORICUS, although this appears to correspond largely with the next route.

HABITOS DE UN PERTURBO IRREMERSIBLE   ***   6c   (E4 6a) 150ft

A "big pitch" in every meaning of the expression.

To the right of the start of GENERATION EXPONTANEA is a bolt line that initially runs straight up the cliff and then veers away to the left. Climb directly up the fluted wall with increasing difficulty to intersect a leftward trending crack line. Follow this on mostly good holds then make more hard moves to a resting place close to where the previous route swings in from the left. Climb up and right via a series of large holds (and no bolts!) until it is possible to trend back left to rejoin the bolt ladder. The steep grey wall is the final obstacle. Continue directly up this to the cliff top or from the end of the difficulties traverse left to the cable in the cave as for the previous two routes.

LA PREGIERO TONTAS/GAMES MOYA *** 6c (E4 6a) 150ft

A direct start combined with the top pitch of GAMES MOYA provides another brilliant way up the cliff with both technical and bold climbing.

To the right of the last route and just beyond a spikey bush is a flat wall running up to a shallow scoop in a band of steeper rock. This should not be confused with a deeper groove further to the right. The wall and scoop give sustained climbing until the rock begins to bulge. Move right slightly to large pockets then attack the leaning wall above with conviction. A fierce pull on small fingerholds gains jugs then easier but distinctly run out climbing (a belief that the climbing is not going to turn tough again is needed) leads straight up the wall to a large hold containing a couple of old threads. From a possible belay here finish much more easily to the left or the right.

GAMES MOYA 6a+ (E2 5c) 60ft

The rather floral groove above the right end of the ledge system is the original start to GAMES MOYA but this is rather redundant now with the start described above. It is climbed to pass a bulge and reach a small stance and bolt belays. Lower off or do the top pitch which lies diagonally up to the left, ** 6c (E4 6a).

OBSESION PERMA NENTE *** E4 170ft

Two pitches of immaculate wall climbing. To the right of the shallow groove of GAMES MOYA is a fine grey face that this route swaggers directly up the centre of.

1. 70ft   6b+ (6a).   From a single bolt belay at edge of the drop to the lower cliff move right onto the face and climb straight up superb rock past a bulge to a small but comfortable stance. A sustained pitch.

2. 100ft   6c   (6a).   Continue in the same line by more sustained climbing up the gradually steepening face. A superb pitch, never desperate but never easy.

ARANA MECHANICA * 6b+ (E3 6a) 50ft
To the right of OBSESION is another bolt line on the smooth grey face. This gives a pleasant but sadly short-lived exercise to the stance at the end of Pitch 3 of PACO EUGENE. Lower off.

The next two routes offer long and sustained climbs on perfect rock (is it ever otherwise), but feel a little unbalanced because of the relatively easy nature of their shared first pitch.

NIRVANA ** E4 160ft
A good route with a tough second pitch of gradually escalating difficulty.
Start by scrambling down (carefully) to a bolt belay to the left of the prominent curving crack that bounds the right side of the smoothest section of the face. NOTE: This can be used as an alternative start to the classic PACO EUGENE thus removing the need to carry any nuts.
1. 60ft   5   (5a).   Climb the crack which proves to be quite beefy to reach a good ledge with belays on the right.
2. 100ft   6b+   (6a).   Step left and climb straight up the wall by sustained but reasonable moves to the foot of some thin cracks. These prove to be considerably more taxing and are climbed by laybacking and thin finger jamming to reach horizontal breaks. Continue to the top more easily. A pumpy pitch.

RONO Y AN EXTRAPLOMA ** E4 170ft
1. 60ft   5   (5a).   As for the first pitch of NIRVANA to the good stance and bolt belays.
2. 110ft   6c   (6a).   Move right along the ledge to the foot of a leaning wall. This is climbed strenuously until it is possible to pull out left to rest in a big hole. Continue up a much easier crack line to ledges and a massive ring belay. Escape to the left along the cables.

Below and right of the large curving crack that forms the first pitch of NIRVANA is a short clean wall with double overhangs below it. This smooth orange wall offers two good face climbs, short in stature but action packed. Both of these start from bolt belays on a small ledge below the twin bulges. This ledge is most easily reached from below but can also be approached by a careful scramble (or an easy abseil) from above. The top pitches of NIRVANA or RONO Y AN EXTRAPLOMA provide a logical continuation to these route if you want to make it to the cliff top, either of these combinations providing a three-star outing, otherwise lower back to the stance below the overhangs.

URBI ET ORDI * 7a (E4 6a) 70ft

The left-hand line. Cross the bulges and climb the wall until forced left onto the arête. Pull back to the right onto the wall and continue to a small ledge and lowering belays. Bale out or move right for a touch of NIRVANA.

LOS COCODRILOS NO LLORAN * 7a+ (E5 6a)

The right-hand line. Difficult pulls through the bulges lead on to the base of the wall. This gives sustained climbing on small sharp holds and on a pocket guaranteed to leave an impression on at least one of your fingers. Lower off from the twin bolts or move up and right for RONO Y AN EXTRAPLOMA.

PACO EUGENE *** E1 320ft

A fine long climb taking a devious but natural line up the highest part of the cliff with a cracking crux pitch high on the wall. There is little fixed gear on the first two pitches and anybody who is intent on having a total break from British ethics and protection may want to start up the first pitch of NIRVANA at 5a (5). Otherwise carry a selection of wires and a couple of slings.

Start at the left edge of the level ground below the cliff below a sheet of grey rock with two prominent bolt runners in it.

1. 70ft 5 (5a). Climb up to the bolts and pass them rightwards by a couple of tricky moves to gain good jugs that lead back to the left. Continue more easily to reach a cleaned ledge on the right. Nut belays.
2. 80ft 4 (4c). Move back left and climb steep flake cracks (peg runner) to deeper cracks. These are followed (threads) to easier ground and then ledges. Move left to the belay on NIRVANA.
3. 30ft 3 (4a). Walk (or teeter) to the left end of the ledge

and reverse mantelshelf off it. Traverse up and left to ledges and bolt belays.

4. 50ft 5 (5a). Climb steeply up to the right to gain a groove which is followed more easily to a cosy stance in a niche below a barrier of overhangs.

5. 90ft 6a (5b). Traverse the difficult slab leftwards (peg and huge jug to clip it from above the roof) to reach a long crack line. This is followed with interest and occasional difficult moves to a final awkward corner and the cliff top. Escape left via the wire cables and with a growing feeling of self satisfaction.

The final two routes are to be found on the south-facing wall that forms the right side of the cliff, "down by the riverside". This face is most easily reached from the COTOS BAJAS. Descending to it from the ledges below the upper section of the Polverin is not recommended.

To the left of the centre of the face is an impressive bulging red corner. This is:

EL ENGRENDO ** 5+ (E1 5b) 90ft
A strenuous pitch on which it might be worth carrying a few middle sized and large nuts.

Climb a short steep wall (crux) to a ledge then move left into the main corner. This is followed in rather brutish style past bolts, pegs and a clutch of bulges up some of the world's roughest rock to a block. Move up and right to a small stance and twin belays. Either abseil off from here or bushwhack up and right then back left to join and finish up PACO EUGENE.

JAQUIMA ** 6b+ (E3 6a) 80ft
Start at a grey slab running up to the base of a colourful leaning wall to the right of the steep corner of the previous route.

Climb the slab easily until the angle changes. The leaning wall is taken by exhilarating moves on a series of massive holds until just short of success. Like everything in life, it is never that simple, and so a battle is required to reach the slab. Poor layaways and small holds are all that is offered by the final leaning wall, though a finger jug hidden in a shallow groove high on the right might be of material assistance. The twin lowering bolts are well over on the left, don't pump out before you clip them.

EL INVENTO, LOS BLOQUES AND EL MAKINODROMO

Character

EL INVENTO, LOS BLOQUES and EL MAKINODROMO are names used for different sections of a continuous edge, more than a kilometre in length, running up the hillside, roughly midway between the upper and lower gorges. From a distance the cliff is dwarfed by the massive crags behind it, but on closer inspection the scale of the edge is very impressive. Only three fairly minor sections have been developed to date, with the majority of the most impressive stretches of the cliff not yet touched. There are superb leaning walls and some magnificent groove lines that are crying out to be climbed, and doubtless they will be when the locals get round to it.

The cliff faces south and is well sheltered from winds that blow through the gorge. Most of the routes that exist at the moment are short (or very short) and steep, almost gritstone like in nature, though with the luxury of bolts and fixed belays. Amongst these small fry is one route of international significance, LOURDES has to be seen to be believed, it makes Dominatrix look like the Idwal Slabs, and should be a destination for pilgrims in search of the ultimate pump.

Access

A bit of a hike, especially to the upper sections of the cliff! Marginally the shortest walk in is via the upper gorge and its Walkway though of course you have to drive round to the upper lakes if you are stopping in El Chorro. Follow the directions for LAS BANERAS and continue through the gorge on the Walkway. Cross the footbridge at PETIT DESFILADERO and walk through the next tunnel to arrive below the lower end of the line of cliffs.

From ALBERCONES or the station follow directions to EL POLVERIN and continue along the track for a couple of hundred metres to an iron bridge which is surprisingly close to the ground. This approach meets the one described above where it emerges from the railway tunnel. About twenty minutes walk should be sufficient from either end to this point. EL INVENTO is the lower section of cliff just above the track and is reached by a short steep scramble. LOS BLOQUES is five minutes arduous walk further up the hill at a series of gigantic boulders and EL MAKINODROMO is the unmistakable leaning wall another fifteen minutes flog up the slope from here. If you are heading from this upper section there is a good footpath well out from the cliff, making for much easier progress though a scramble along the foot of the cliff is impressive in the extreme.

The routes are described from left to right as they are approached from the railway line.

El Invento

The first routes are a collection of tiny pitches at the left end of the cliff. If the first ascensionists could have been bothered to walk a little further they could have created some real classics just a short distance up the hill.

FRESQUITO GRESQUITO 6c (E3 6a) 20ft
The bulging left arête of the cliff gives a short and rather unsatisfying struggle.

ME EMPINO CON UN CHUMINO 6b (E1 6a) 30ft
Battle round the white bulge just to the right to gain a sloping ledge and bolt. Continue up a groove (thread, not insitu) to the twin-bolt belay.

To the right is steep smooth slab which is climbed by:

DISCORDIA * 6b (E3 6a) 40ft
Climb straight up to the first bolt on small holds and continue by more thin moves to the top of the slab. Step left and continue more easily to chains.

Right again is a leaning groove leading to an impressive bulging arête.

ALUCINA POR LA ESQUINA   *   7b+   50ft
The initial groove gives a tricky start, but the arête provides the meat of the route, being sustained, technical and strenuous, as well as set at a quite ridiculous angle.

To the right is a leaning orange wall and steep smooth corner before a section of easier angled rock that should provide some good climbing at amenable grades. At present it is undeveloped. To the right again is a left-facing open groove with a crack in its back.

DIEDRE VENENO   *   6a   (E1 5b)   50ft
Climb the groove with sustained interest. The belays are fixed but not much else is, so carry a selection of large nuts and Friends.

Up and round to the right is a flat area below a bulging wall which is split by a fiercely overhanging thin crack line. To its left is a line of bolts running up a bulging wall:

LA LECHE QUE MAMASTE   **   7b+   50ft
Follow the line with considerable difficulty and a long move left to reach a glacis. Cross the bulge blindly and then trend left to the belays, a real pumper.

AHORA, AHORA QUE TE PILLO SOLA   **   7a+   40ft
The crack line gives another workout for your forearms and offers some exquisitely painful finger locks which are used to reach "real" jams and then easier climbing.

Right again is more ignored but eminently climbable rock with some excellent looking lines. Thirty metres to the right and just beyond a large solitary tree is a bulging wall containing some large bolts.

SABINOROYAL   **   6b+   (E4 6a)   70ft
Improvise past the first bolt especially if you are short then head

straight up the wall with a tricky bulge and at least one "gripper clipper".

Fifty metres further up the slope and just before a patch of thorn bushes is:

PANTOMIMAS 6b+ (E2 6a) 30ft
Step in from the right and climb a short leaning wall to easier rock and a nice shiny belay.

To the right is a low blackened recess, the left wall of which provides two pitches.

ESCLAVO DE GRADO 6c+ (E4 6a) 40ft
The left-hand line is followed on painful finger pockets first left and then back right.

LA TOMAS A LO DEJOS 7b 40ft
The right-hand line is fierce and technical with more painful pocket pulling.

Up and round to the right is a large orange flake perched close to the rock. Starting from the foot of this is:

CHAPAMONIA 6c+ (E4 6b) 40ft
Swing out left onto a ledge then scale the leaning grey wall to ledge and twinned bolts.

LA VIA SHING 6b (E3 6a) 40ft
Up and right is a vegetated corner. Start up this then swing left into a thin crack and follow it over a bulge to the top.

To the right is a short grey slab behind bushes. The left side of this is climbed by:

PERIPECIAS DE INVALIDO 6c (E2 6a) 30ft
Short and sharp climbing passing two bolt runners.

To the right of the bushes is a thirty-foot-high triangular flake. Starting at the bottom left edge of this is:

NACIDA PARA LA CRITICA * 6c+ (E4 6a) 40ft
Swing onto the leaning wall and climb it to more amenable angled rock. Trend leftwards to the belays.

The next two routes are rather short exercises starting from a rather gripping position on the tip of the triangular pointed flake. They are tough but trivial.

HEMOGLOBINA 6b (E2 6a) 20ft
The left-hand line.

JUEGO DURO 6c (E3 6b) 20ft
The right-hand and steeper line.

Los Bloques

Continuing up the hillside for five minutes or so one reaches an area where a series of colossal chunks have fallen from the cliff and shattered into a series of blocks big enough to dwarf the Bowder Stone or the Cromlech boulders. There are two routes on the main face and another on one of the larger boulders.

Before a rift formed by a great tilted block are two pitches worth seeking out.

COMICOS Y MODISTAS * 6b+ (E3 6a) 50ft
The left-hand line gives a pleasantly sustained pitch on good but occasionally spaced flowstone holds with the crux reserved for the final moves.

STRAW DONKEY ** 7c 60ft
The right-hand line is a whole different ball game, uphill and overhanging, mean and muscular, do(g) it or fly.

Immediately in front of the previous two routes is a block with a severely overhanging front face. This is taken by:

LA TETE DE MARI   8b   40ft
A tough cookie especially considering its diminutive size.

According to the local top another of the blocks hereabouts contains three routes from 6a to 6b+ but a search of the area has not located them. Any budding Livingstones out there fancy exploring this bit of snake territory?

El Makinodromo

The final routes are fifteen minutes flog further up the hill (twenty minutes from the railway) where a grossly leaning wall is to be found. It is festooned with stalactites and shelters a large goat pen. The ground below the cliff is dust-dry up to fifty feet out from the foot of the wall, this truly is a cliff that never gets wet. At the moment it contains one solitary line though with an eye of faith there is room for a lot more. Perhaps a future playground for the muscle bound?

Starting ten feet right of a solitary tree against the rock is:

LOURDES   ***   8a+   140ft
An awkward couple of first moves gives access to "bucket city". Romp on to a substantial roof and do battle with this then continue with more sustained difficulties up the never-ending overhanging wall. If successful lower off to land fifty feet out from your starting place. If not, pull the ropes and try all over again. A UK grade of (E7 6a) has been mooted for this pitch, impressive numbers for an impressive pitch.

The final selection of climbs are 130 metres further around to the right. Here there are several short but tough pitches. They may be of use if you have walked up to do LOURDES and don't quite feel up to the task in hand or if you found it easy and want a few "quickies" to finish off the day.

The first route starts just right of a tree at a "tufa" pillar.

LA EPOCA EM ** 7b 60ft
The initial leaning wall is a bit of a battle, the big roof presents rather more of a challenge.

Thirty metres to the right is a ledge at ten feet with COTO painted in large white letters.

GANTO PECADO ** 7b 70ft
From the left end of the ledge climb the wall to a ledge then attack the leaning rock above with conviction.

ONE BASTION B.A. ** 7b+ 70ft
From the centre of the ledge climb to a higher ledge then do battle with the orange streak on the tilted wall above.

POST FESTUM * 7a+ 70ft
Up a crack at the right side of the ledge then the wall just left of the hanging arête above.

Immediately to the right of a bush at twenty feet is a line with its name painted on the rock, this is:

MEGA FLASH ** 7b 70ft
Climb up to a ledge then step left on to the leaning wall. Improvise around the roof to a ledge, the belays are a little higher.

CRUMEL EL CURTDOR *** 7a 70ft
Start as for MEGA FLASH and continue up the bulging corner until it is possible to exit to the right. Trend back left to reach the belays of the previous climb.

PUNK STREET ** 7a 80ft
Start at the name painted on the rock and climb the steep initial wall into a cosy hollow. When suitably refreshed get stuck into the bulging wall above.

To the right the good rock continues for a considerable distance. The existence of cultivated terraces on the hillside opposite this final area suggest that there is some form of vehicle access to these upper slopes. The local military map does not mark any tracks in the vicinity, but if you are intent on a siege on LOURDES it might be worth doing a bit of geographical research to save yourself the hike up each day.

PETIT DESFILADERO

Character

A mini ravine (at least when compared to the upper and lower gorges though it is not really all that mini) spanned by a decrepit bridge and with the river Guadalhorce cascading through the bottom. The rock consists mainly of water-worn scoops and bulges and the climbing tends to be steep, fierce and fingery. All the routes are well bolted, and it would appear to make good sense to place the quick draws as you abseil in wherever possible. There is only a small collection of pitches here and they are generally quite tough. Despite this there is a lot of scope for new routing at amenable grades.

All but one of the routes listed is approached by abseil and the bolts at the top of these climbs means that they can be top roped easily (the top roping is easy, getting up the climbs is less so). If you decide to abseil in and pull your ropes down a considerable degree of self-confidence is required. It is possible to escape from the bottom of the ravine by heading upstream, but such an action would almost certainly lead at very best to wet feet.

Access

Follow the directions to reach the upper gorge (fifteen minutes drive from El Chorro) and follow the Walkway past Las Baneras to where the gorge opens out. Continue along the Walkway to where a peculiar "upside down" bridge spans the ravine, and a much abused little house is to be found on the right, sheltering under the cliff. The routes all lie within fifty metres of this bridge. Ten minutes from the car.

I have included a map to locate the routes and information on grades, lengths and quality. All the names are painted at the top of the climbs and so further description is superfluous.

NOTE: Access to the abseil bolts above some of the routes on the northern side of the ravine is a little tricky. Care is required unless

PETIT DESFILADERO

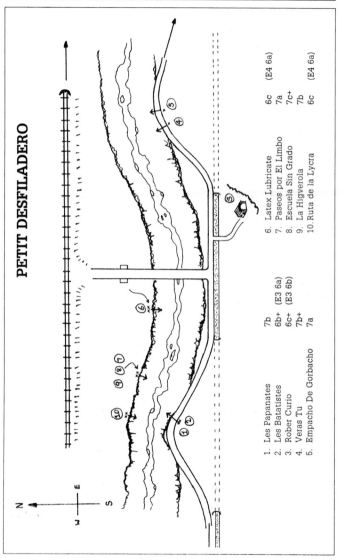

1. Les Papanates   7b
2. Les Batatistes   6b+   (E3 6a)
3. Rober Curio   6c+   (E3 6b)
4. Veras Tu   7b+
5. Empacho De Gorbacho   7a

6. Latex Lubricate   6c   (E4 6a)
7. Paseos por El Limbo   7a
8. Escuela Sin Grado   7c+
9. La Higverola   7b
10. Ruta de la Lycra   6c   (E4 6a)

you are after an Acapulco-type diving session.

On the south (Walkway) side the routes are listed as they are approached when walking downstream.

On the Walkway a short distance after the water channel disappears into a tunnel and just around an arête are twin bolts. These give access to:

LES PAPANATES *** 7b, 5+ 140ft
The upstream line. Steep to the point of being ridiculous!

LES BATATISLES *** 6b+, 4 (E3 6a, 4b) 140ft
The downstream line proves to be considerably more amenable.

Behind the little house is:

ROBER CURIO * 6c+ (E3 6b) 50ft
Short, sharp and sadly smelly.

Just before the Walkway round the next arête going downstream are two single bolts. The first one gives access to:

VERAS TU *** 7b+ 120ft
A very impressive pitch.

The second bolt lets you get at:

EMPACHO DE GORBACHO *** 7a 120ft
Not as fierce as its near neighbour but another tough cookie.

The remaining routes are on the north (railway) side of the gorge. They are listed as they are approached from the bridge, ie. walking upstream.

Just west of the bridge a short scramble leads down to the top of:

LATEX LUBRICATE ** 6c (E4 6a)
Scoopy climbing to a rather dirty exit. A route for lovers of safe manoeuvres.

Thirty metres further to the west are twin bolts that are below the cliff top and are rather difficult to locate from above. Checking their position from the other side first is a good idea. APPROACH

THEM WITH CARE. These bolts facilitate a ninety-foot abseil to a bay from which three good routes make their separate ways back to the belays.

PASEOS POR EL LIMBO *** 7a 90ft
The right-hand and most reasonable line.

ESCUELA SIN GRADO *** 7c+ 80ft
The central line, steep scoopy and exceedingly technical.

LA HIGVEROLA ** 7b 80ft
The left-hand line, more scallopy climbing.

A little further upstream is the final pair of bolts. An abseil from these leads to the base of:

RUTA DE LA LYCRA *** 6c (E4 6a) 90ft
A pitch consisting of alternating bulges and hollows. The rock is interestingly sculptured as well.

LAS BANERAS

Character

The upper gorge cut by the Guadalhorce at El Chorro is deep, narrow and very impressive. Imagine Huntsman's Leap five times as deep and half as wide, then stick a footpath halfway up one side! The rock is impeccable and protection is plentiful and includes substantial lowering points. All the pitches described lie above or below the Walkway on the southern wall of the rift. There is also a collection of fine looking pitches on the opposite wall. These are approached by abseiling into the "pit" and crossing the rift on one or other of a variety of wire cables that span the gap well above the bottom to reach the other side. I have not done any of these routes though they look very worthwhile. The rather vague topo at the Station Bar suggests that there are at least eight climbs here varying in grade from 6a+ to 7b+ and from one to three pitches in length. The area looks well worth a visit though remember that at the end of the day's climbing you have to re-cross the cables and get back up to the Walkway, save a little strength.

In winter there is often a cold wind blowing through the defile, though calm days can be climbable here. On the other hand in high summer the shady depths of the "hole" provide the opportunity of cool climbing for cool dudes.

Access

By car. From El Chorro cross the dam and turn right. Follow the rather poor road uphill through cowboy country for six kilometres until it improves dramatically at a road junction. Turn right and continue for two kilometres to a right turn just before a tunnel and a pleasant bar (worth checking out on the way home). A dirt road is followed first uphill and then down through a tunnel to ample parking outside the hydroelectric power station, ten to fifteen minutes drive from El Chorro. Pass round the fence and take the track that descends to the left of the buildings. The climbing is three minutes walk away along the horizontal path, just beyond the old gate.

By foot. Follow the directions to El Polverin and continue over the black iron bridge and through the next tunnel. On emerging from this turn left and cross the rickety bridge at the Petit Desfiladeros. Turn right and follow the Walkway up into the ever-more impressive jaws of the gorge. Fifty minutes walk from the station.

The routes are described from right to left as this is the usual direction of approach. Many of them have their names painted on the rock though these works of art are often faded. The first climbs are on a light-coloured slab that rises from the Walkway, seventy metres beyond the gateway and memorial plaque at the start of the suspended part of the Walkway.

MEMBRILLO ** 5 (HVS 5a) 70ft
A pleasant pitch. Climb the slab on sharp holds until it begins to steepen up. Follow the ramp leftwards then make a couple of steeper moves on good holds to the belay bolts.

To the left is a steeper line of fixed gear running up to join the previous route a short distance below the chains. To the left of the start are a pair of substantial belay bolts.

HIJO PUT EL QUITE LAS CHAPAS ** 5+ (E1 5b) 70ft
Climb up and slightly right to good pockets from where more difficult moves lead slightly leftwards across a smoother section. Better holds lead straight up to the belays.

Five metres left are two bolts linked by a wire cable. This is the belay for a seventy-foot abseil to a small ledge below and right of a bush at the start of:

MOLA MAS QUE AMERICA ** 6a+ (E2 5c)
From the ledge move up and right then left past the small bush. Climb a smooth and difficult section before trending right to gain a position below the Walkway. Curse the pigeons and then mantelshelf wildly back to freedom. A route that offers an interesting insight into "the hole" and the potential available down there.

Fourteen metres further to the left is an orange bay where the Walkway opens out and it is possible to escape from that frightening drop. The bay is the starting point of two fine climbs.

REPLICANDO Y CON EL MAZO DANDO *** 8a 90ft
An awesome pitch up the right side of the bay. Hard climbing leads into a depression, followed by more of the same up a leaning wall. The angle and the difficulties gradually relent if you have the wherewithal to keep going.

A GOLPE DE MAZO *** 7b+ 90ft
Climb up the left side of the bay then swing back to the right and make steep and difficult moves to gain the marginally easier wall above. This gives fine sustained climbing to the belays.

Around to the left the Walkway widens at a small walled alcove jutting out over the drop. Here is:

ALGO SOBELA VIRGIN *** 6a+ (E3 5c) 90ft
Climb over the bulges and up right onto the smooth rib which is tackled by a couple of tricky moves to reach a steeper wall. The pockets on this are large but spaced, except for one section where they are small and spaced. Steeper moves on "biffos" gains the belays. Great climbing.

Below the walled alcove is a bolt line with the final bolt set in the brickwork. This would appear to be an escape route from climbs on the other side of the gorge. This may be FINIS BLEU 6b+ (E3 6a).

To the left of the walled alcove is a rib leading to a large pocket and then steeper rock. This is the line of:

EL PERRO VIOLADAR * 6b+ (E3 6a) 50ft
Climb to the left of the initial overhang then trend right to gain the large pocket. A short, sharp leaning section leads to better holds and the belays.

Continuing along the Walkway, the next bolt line starts just to the right of a small ramp that slopes up to the left.

SIN COLUMPIARSE ** 7a+ 70ft
Steep fingery climbing leads to a hanging flake. Up this by powerful moves then bear away to the left to reach the belays.

Ten metres left from the ramp are a collection of shorter pitches. A pair of large black bolts at ten feet can be used as a belay or abseil anchor. Clip them by climbing (carefully) onto the railings. To the right of the paired bolts is:

AL VERDON COM UN MELON 6a+ (E2 6a) 40ft
Climb the wall rightwards to reach ledges.

An eighty-foot abseil from the paired black bolts leads down a fine water-washed scoop with a seasonal pool at its base. This is reclimbed by:

TUBULAR BELLS *** 6c+ (E4 6b) 80ft
A brilliant pitch offering bridging wide enough to make most mortals squeal.
Step right and climb above the pool by sustained "stemming" until it is possible to escape on the right rib and put your hips back into their sockets. Step back into the scoop then climb it and the thin wall to gain the underside of the Walkway. Mantelshelf to safety.

Back on the Walkway and running up left from the paired bolts is a line of black bolts running up the wall passing to the right of a big hole at ten feet. These form the protection on:

EL PERITO CALIANTE * 6b (E3 6a) 40ft
A short fingery pitch not without technical interest.

EL ROBO DEL SIGLO * 6b+ (E3 6a) 40ft
To the left a line of silver bolts rises to the right to reach the same belay. A little tougher than its near neighbour.

Left again is a slight orange bay with a route starting up its back wall.

PINCHITO MORUNO ** 6c (E4 6a) 60ft
More steep and fingery wall climbing, with the occasional good pocket thrown in for good measure.

EL IMPERIO DE LOS SENTIOS ** 6c (E4 6a) 60ft
Start a little further to the left and trend right up the wall to a belay shared with the previous route.

Six metres further along the Walkway is a large hollow at twenty feet, this is crossed by:

MOROSIOPUTA ** 6c+ (E4 6b) 70ft
Climb into the hollow then continue by fine but difficult climbing up the leaning wall above.

Ten metres left past a bay is a long line of bolts running up the wall and over the centre of a wide roof before continuing up a rib. The pitch looks fine and hard though no details are known.

The final route in this area is to be found twenty-five metres further to the left, and twelve metres to the right of where a set of steps leads down to a lower level. Start below and right of a fine groove line.

ASPOMANTIS *** 5 (HVS 5a) 100ft
Climb up awkward slanting ledges to the foot of the corner. This is followed throughout via fine sustained bridging and laybacking to some blocks with the belay bolts out on the right wall of the corner. The slab and groove that run on upwards from the belay look super, go to it.

On the other side of the gorge are some very impressive overhangs with the odd piece of gear visible in spectacular situations. To the right the cliffs approach a thousand feet in height (I kid you not), and an easy angled ridge runs up to meet a steeper groove line which runs to the cliff top. It looks like a classic there for the asking, any takers?

Continuing along the Walkway the path descends then just before it rounds a corner there is a wall on the right with pronounced diagonal cracks rising across it from right to left. There are three pleasant routes here that totally ignore the structure of the rock and climb straight up the cliff. Again they are described from right to left.

EL PODER DE UN SOLA DIOS * 5 (HVS 5a) 60ft
The right-hand line involves a tricky little roof early on then gives pleasant climbing past an orange flake with a bit of a stretch for the belay chains.

JOYAS MEDIOS ** 5 (HVS 5a) 80ft
The central line starts from the foot of the steps and fires straight up the wall by sustained and superbly well protected climbing. Nine bolt runners.

IZQUIERDO CAMINO * 5+ (E1 5b) 80ft
The left-hand line slants left past a metal spike to reach the first bolt then trends rightwards up the wall with the crux moves passing the overlap. This is easiest on the right and requires a long reach. Easier climbing remains.

EL TORCAL DE ANTEQUERA

Character

El Torcal is a small national park a few kilometres to the south of the large town of Antequera, thirty kilometres north of Malaga. It is a high limestone peak (rising to over 4,200 feet or 1,300m) that displays classic "karst" scenery, with clints and grykes, limestone pavements, dry valleys and cave entrances. The top of the peak is basically a heavily dissected plateau of horizontally layered limestone beds. The extensive erosion here has produced many thousands of pinnacles of all shapes and sizes many of which presumably have never been climbed. Between the towers and spires there are lush valleys and verdant depressions containing a fine variety of plant life.

The height of the mountains means that it can be very cool here in winter if you are exposed to the winds and the locals have a saying that if there is a cloud anywhere in Spain it will be over Torcal. Despite this (don't worry it's not true) when the sun shines the place is truly beautiful, well worth getting to know. The altitude gives a special quality to the air and it is a great place to get a rapid sun tan, well away from the polluted atmosphere of the coastal plain. From every summit it is possible to spy out more and more bizzare towers in all directions and in the distance the high tops of the Sierra Nevada can be seen with their snow slopes glistening in the winter sunshine.

Close to the car park is a large building, the lower floor of which houses a display about the surrounding area. It offers an interesting insight into the geology, flora and fauna of the park and is well worth a walk round. Within the park there is a variety of circular waymarked footpaths that start from the car park in the centre of the park and provide gentle exercise in great surroundings and a chance to marvel at the geology (see map). If you decide to leave the footpaths make sure that you know where you last saw a marker, Hampton Court Maze has got nothing on this place!

Camping is allowed in a couple of the depressions to the north-east of the car park and water is available from the toilets in the visitors' centre when it is open. At other times of the year it will need to be brought up from either Villanueva de la Concepcion just to the south or from Antequera a little further away to the north.

The established routes are concentrated in a few scattered and small areas. It is almost as if the locals, daunted by the amount of rock available, have picked a couple of discrete places to develop in an attempt to find their feet. Almost all of the routes described are bolt-protected and have good anchors to lower off from on top of the pinnacles. The scope for new routing and pinnacle bashing is endless as is the bouldering potential, though please try to remember that the place is a national park so use a little bit of discretion.

Because of the nature of the erosion that has taken place the actual style of the climbing is rather strange, often consisting of long reaches between sloping holds or making progress using side pulls in the many horizontal breaks. It may take a little getting used to but it is well worth the effort and it may delight any gritstone gurus who are feeling a little homesick.

Access

El Torcal can be approached direct from Malaga by following the rather tortuous road north towards Antequera. This divides after ten kilometres. Either take the left fork which passes through the town of Almogia to reach Villanueva de la Concepcion (passing El Chaparral, keep an eye out for Indians). Or alternatively take the slightly shorter but more twisty right-hand fork to the same place. From here the road towards Antequera climbs steadily eventually to reach a sharp left turn into the park. Follow the road uphill, keeping left to reach the car park on the roof of the known world (approximately forty kilometres, an easy hour's drive).

If you are without transport it is possible to catch the train from Malaga via El Chorro to Antequera and then hitch the last ten kilometres to the park. Be warned if you get dropped off at the entrance it is a considerable uphill walk to the climbing.

If you are stopping at El Chorro the park can be approached by car in about forty-five minutes by a drive that offers some interesting insights into the country hereabouts. Take the dirt road that runs uphill from the station and keep left at the first junction. The road rises steeply and passes under LOS ENCANTADAS before reaching

A small section of El Torcal. Go forth and do your own thing

a settlement on a col. Bear left here then follow the road for about eight kilometres. The road contours the hillside then descends gently, passing some impressive rock, to reach the town of Valle de Abdalais. Just short of the town is a road closed sign. This has been in place for several years and can be safely ignored. Now continue north on a tarmacked road (such luxury) which then swings round and heads east. After eighteen kilometres, and just short of the fleshpots of Antequera there is a road junction. Turn right and follow the road uphill steadily for eight kilometres until the park entrance is reached. The road rises steadily until it passes through a gap on the rocks and then descends gently to the car park on top of the mountain.

The Climbs

The first few routes described are to be found by an impressive south-facing bowl of rock that is visible high on the right a short distance after entering the park. These are reached by turning sharp right off the road running up to the top of the hill on another road that runs back towards the transmitter on the eastern top of the ridge. An inconspicuous and bumpy right fork off this leads into a disused marble quarry. There are three worthwhile routes on the natural rock to the right of the quarry, in this rather grotty setting.

EL TORCAL.
Climbing areas and waymarked paths

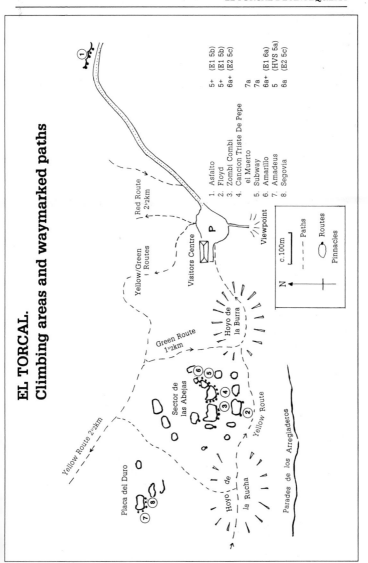

1. Asfalto   5+   (E1 5b)
2. Floyd   5+   (E1 5b)
3. Zombi Combi   6a+   (E2 5c)
4. Cancion Triste De Pepe
      el Muerto   7a
5. Subway   7a
6. Amarillo   6a+   (E1 6a)
7. Amadeus   5   (HVS 5a)
8. Segovia   6a   (E2 5c)

ALICIA QUIMICA * 7a 60ft
Climb the steep wall to the right of the quarried rock to a series of bulges that are crossed by harsh use of small and very sharp holds. Above is a single belay bolt, lower off or traverse right to the twin bolts on the next route.

INVERTIDA * 6c (E3 6a) 60ft
The wall, just right of a blunt arête, gives sustained and intricate climbing. The bolt runners are well camouflaged, but are all there.

At the back right side of the steep bowl of rock is an impressive ragged crack line:

ME NOMBRE ES NINQUNO ** 8a 70ft
If you enjoy steep sustained painful climbing with a minimum of footholds and perfect protection, this is the one for you.

The next collection of routes is to be found on a flat south-facing wall that is passed on the right just before the road levels out, a short distance short of the car park. There are five routes here offering good climbing on compact rock. Park sensibly on the roadside remembering that large coaches occasionally pass this way. The cliff is basically a broad wall split into thirds by two vertical cracks. The climbs were all originally aid routes and still contain remnants from these early ascents. They are described from left to right. The first feature is a thin finger crack near the left edge of the buttress:

BUFONES * 6b (E3 5c) 40ft
The crack gives a pleasant but short-lived piece of finger jamming to reach a single lowering bolt on the rib.

TORQUELLE * 7a 70ft
Start from a pile of flakes on the left side of the cliff. Climb over a bulge and follow a short crack to its end. Continue up the centre of the wall with sustained difficulty to a horizontal break. Continue more easily to the top.

The left-hand crack is unclimbed at present but should give someone a pleasant HVS. The wall between the two cracks is tackled by:

Chris Craggs on the classic ASFALTO 5+ (E1 5b), El Torcal

ANTEQUERA ANTIK *** 7b 80ft

Climb to a bulge and pass it with great difficulty. The smooth wall above proves to be sustained and highly technical, but eases as height is gained.

ASFALTO *** 5+ (E1 5b) 80ft

The characteristic twisting diedre in the centre of the cliff is gained by a couple of steep moves and is then followed throughout by pleasant bridging and the occasional layback move. The fixed protection is good but rather spaced so it may be worth carrying a few nuts. Lowering bolts are available above the final crack.

DOMINGUEROS CRACK ** 6c (E5 6b) 80ft

The line starting just right of the previous climb has a tough initial bulge and then eases a little before rearing up into a hard upper section up a discontinuous crack line in the bulging arête. The Spanish grade is a bit on the mean side.

The rest of the developed areas are approached from the main car park, and are reached by a five-minute stroll. The first area reached is known as:

Sector de las Abejas

Access

Walk west, passing directly in front of the visitors' centre and follow the green path in reverse. (The other path which goes off at a tangent runs out to a viewpoint offering extensive panoramas to the south as far as the distant blue Mediterranean.) After passing through a depression, La Hoyo de la Burra, the path rises and forks rather inconspicuously. The left branch is the Yellow Path in reverse, though the first arrow on it is in fact a green one. It is followed over a hill and down through a narrow flat valley with a long dark north-facing cliff (Paredes de los Arregladeros) on the left. This cliff contains two routes at present: a smooth bolted wall right of centre, and a long groove sprouting the odd peg, further to the right. Because the cliff faces north it is not a popular winter venue, though if you are in the area in the summer it may be worthy of further attention.

The SECTOR DE LAS ABEJAS is on the right here, five minutes from the car providing that you do not get lost. The geography of the area is rather complex (see map). The first four routes are on the highest pinnacle to the right of the path and its near neighbour to the left, and the rest are to be found tucked away behind these. These first four routes are described from right to left, ie. as they are passed on the footpath.

The first route is a two-pitch climb on the highest pinnacle. It is recognised by the crack splitting the upper tower and the large flat roof low down. Start on the ledge below the roof.

LA CONJURA DE LOS RECIOS ** E4 100ft
1. 60ft   6c   (6a).   Climb the wall to the crack that splits the right side of the roof using a "naughty" finger pocket then battle round the overhang to reach easier ground. Romp onto a good ledge and two-bolt belay.
2. 40ft   6a   (5c).   Follow the fine steep crack in the headwall to twin bolts just below the summit of the tower. After planting your flag lower off, or belay on the top and scramble down the back (Diff).

Around to the left is a flaky corner with a blue cross and some writing painted twenty feet up its right wall. This forms the first pitch of:

FLOYD * E1 100ft
Carry a selection of wires for the top pitch unless you trust pegs with twisted wire loops to clip into.
1. 60ft   5   (5a).   Follow the fine flaky corner past two bolts to a ledge at its top. Climb up and left to a belay below a thin crack in the steep headwall of the tower.
2. 40ft   5+   (5b).   The thin slanting finger crack is tough but short-lived, the fixed pegs are museum pieces and should be respected as such. From the top of the tower the safest and easiest way down is to scramble off to the north (Diff).

To the left are a couple of large trees and around to the left of these are two worthwhile climbs on a west-facing wall. The first one follows a prominent flake. Carry a selection of runners.

PETETE * 4 (VS 4b) 60ft
Follow the fine flake passing a peg to a ledge at its top. Climb up to a higher ledge with a bolt and continue on to the top of the tower with a far away look in your eye. Scramble over the top to belay and descend via an awkward groove.

To the left is a narrow buttress with a thin crack splitting a set of three bulges. This is:

ATOMIC * 6a+ (E2 5c) 40ft
The bolts are rather spaced so carry a few wires or blast up the crack. The moves are a touch butch but good holds keep appearing as long as you have the "umph" to use them. A ledge with twin bolts is your reward, lower off.

A small pinnacle some distance in front of the last two routes contains two short climbs on its north side. The left one climbs a wall into the base of a crack and contains a well hidden peg and bolt, whilst the right one climbs the wall past two bolts. The Spanish grades are 5 and 5+ respectively though these may need treating with a bit of caution.

The next climbs are to be found in the best developed area, and lie just across the grassy bay to the north of the previous routes. Either cut across a rocky platform to reach them or continue along the Yellow Path for a short distance until it is possible to walk round behind the pinnacles just described. Here there is a fine collection of walls facing in a variety of direction, but especially southwards.

The climbs on the mains walls are described from left to right. Forty metres to the left of the main tower is a small pinnacle with one short route:

COMIC 6c (E4 6a) 30ft
The bulging south face of the tower is climbed past a series of unhelpful horizontal breaks to twin bolts, short and sharp and not very amusing. Lower off.

The main tower is known as the AGRIO DEL ASA and it contains four fine climbs. On the left a slightly shorter tower leans against the main one. The front face of this is tackled by:

LA ABUELITA ROCKERA * 7a 50ft
A steep pitch on a remarkably unhelpful set of holds. Strength, stamina and perhaps a touch of luck are required for a successful on-sight attempt.

To the right is a high tower with two prominent crack lines on it. This is the site of three excellent climbs, and the base of the wall provides a superbly sheltered picnic and sunbathing spot.

NEBLINA PATAGONICA *** 6b+ (E3 5c) 90ft
Gain a steep bulging left-hand crack awkwardly and follow it strenuously to a rest in a cave recess. Exiting from this is awkward though big jugs lurk over the lip to aid the pull over. Easier climbing remains.

CON JOROBA NO SE BLOQUEA ** 6c (E4 6a) 90ft
The bulging arête between the two cracks is followed with sustained interest, or should that read difficulty? Most of the holds are reasonable but some of them take a bit of finding.

ZOMBI COMBI *** 6a+ (E2 5c) 90ft
The right-hand crack is gained from the left across ledges and followed by bridging to a sinister bulge. Swing smartly right under this to gain the finely sculptured groove and follow this easily to the top.

The back of the pinnacle is ascendable by a slabby ridge at V. Diff, a worthwhile trip for the summit views.

To the right is another pinnacle with a collection of routes on its west and south sides. It can be recognised by the giant fallen blocks laid in front of the south face. The first four routes are on the west face of the tower, around to the left of these blocks.

METALICA ** 7a 60ft
The leaning wall to the right of the left arête of the tower gives a

steep and sustained piece of climbing with a goodly selection of big bolt runners. Twin lowering bolts just below the top.

HIERROS ** 6b+ (E3 6a) 60ft
The disappearing crack line is followed to its end from where a couple of difficult moves past two pegs allow a swing right to gain easier ground and a wide elegantly sculpted finishing groove. Belays are to be found in the summit block.

EL MOCO *** 6b (E3 5c) 70ft
The bulging wall to the right of the crack is climbed slightly rightwards to a rest at the foot of the slab. Step left and climb directly on hidden holds before stepping left into the hanging groove of the previous route which provides an easier finish.

DOMINGO SANGRIENTO * (E3 5c) 70ft
To the left of the right arête of the wall is a bulging crack. This is gained from a block on the left and followed steeply to reach a wider section and peg runner. The upper section is easier but has no fixed gear, continue with care or place your own protection.

Around the arête to the right is the south face of the block. This contains three routes.

CANCION TRISTE DE PEPE EL MUERTO *** 7a 70ft
The steep wall just right of the arête is started from the ground and is climbed trending leftwards. It gives a great pitch on small sharp and well spaced fingerholds trending left then straight up. A bit like being back on the climbing wall, but what a setting.

PALOMERAS * 5 (E1 5b) 80ft
Start from the block and drop across the void to gain the wall and a solitary and elderly bolt. The first move to get established is a pig (at least 6a if you are less than 5'10"), the rest is a romp. Take the steep crack (thread, not insitu) then from the ledges climb the corner on the right to the summit of the tower. The belays are over to the left.

BALADA DE CAIN ** 7b+ 60ft
The wall to the left of the right arête of the face gives a short but steep and fierce pitch with a small selection of "chipadeedodas". The hardest route in the area but on uncharacteristically sharp holds. Lower off from a twin peg and single bolt belay.

A short scramble up around the corner and past a narrow rift reveals another wall facing east and with three routes on it. The first one is:

ARBONIATO ** 6c (E3 6b) 50ft
Step into the groove from the right and follow it steeply until an immense reach gains the break. Swing rapidly rightwards then follow much easier rock up into a groove and onto the top of the pinnacle. The belays are over to the right above the next route. The direct finish needs doing, but a Sword of Damocles might need attention first.

SUBWAY * 7a 50ft
The bulging arête to the right of the upper groove is started on the left and followed with escalating difficulty and a gradually increasing angle. An uphill battle with the expected jugs proving to be a touch illusive.

EL ESPOLON ** E3 6a (6b+) 50ft
The right arête of the pinnacle is climbed on its left side and has a tough starting move and then eases to a series of long reaches between good jugs. Passing the final rounded bulge is problematical, try it on the left, or sneak off to the right.

The back wall of the tower has a couple of pleasant pitches.

IZQIUERDO ** 5 (HVS 5a) 50ft
Step off the block used by the previous climb and shoot up the steep wall on good holds. Very pleasant.

DERECHO ** 5 (HVS 5a) 50ft
Climb onto a block in the gully then follow a surprisingly positive set of holds to the top.

On the other side of the gully is the final route in this area. It has two widely spaced bolts in it, one near the bottom and one near the top:

AMARILLO * E1 6a (6a+) 50ft
Passing the first bolt is tough then much easier but run out climbing leads to the second one. Step left and climb the arête, finishing up the front or more easily around to the left.

There is one other route in this area, though it is rather illusive. From the picnic spot at the foot of ZOMBI COMBI walk round to the left to reach the back of the tower. Opposite here is a climb that starts up a south-east-facing corner:

BONZA * 6a (E2 5b) 40ft
Climb the corner past an old bolt then swing onto the steep wall. This is best climbed rapidly, especially as the holds deteriorate as height is gained so pumping out is a real possibility. Lower off.

Placa del Duro

The final area that has been developed is the PLACA DEL DURO. This section of rock contains a small collection of excellent climbs and took me several visits to locate. For this reason I will not apologise for including detailed approach information. If you want a bit of exploring and to do the 'Doctor Livingston, I presume' bit, ignore the next couple of paragraphs.

From below ZOMBI COMBI in the Sector de las Abejas walk west for about seventy metres to the lowest point in the centre of the next large depression, this is the Hoyo de la Rucha. Alternatively continue along the Yellow Path in reverse for the same distance. This should bring you close to a prominent solitary hawthorn tree. Standing by this and with your back to the large dark wall, look due south. The PLACA DEL DURO is the largest visible face and shows pronounced horizontal stratification. It is located behind and left of a tripple-topped pinnacle. The foot of the face is reached by heading up the valley that runs left past this pinnacle until it is possible to scramble up to the right to the foot of the cliff. This approach passes a short compact wall from which the bolts have been removed at the time of writing. These were the Vias de Espelio and no grades for them are available.

The climbs on the PLACA DEL DURO are located on the west and south faces of the tower and are up to 100 feet in height. The summit is one of the highest in the area and the outward views are superb, the place is well worth a visit. There are twin abseil bolts situated above the centre of the south face from where a 100-foot abseil leads to the foot of the face. The routes are described from left to right.

In roughly the centre of the west face is a corner starting from a ledge and with a line of bolts running up its right wall. These provide the substantial protection on:

CHORREOSIS ** E1 100ft
An excellent first pitch.
1. 60ft   6a   (5b).   Start up the corner then trend right to bulges. These are passed using a short finger crack that contains a family of geckos (honestly). Swing left to clip a bolt then trend right up the wall with occasional tricky moves to reach twin ring bolts at a good stance.
2. 40ft   5   (5a).   Step left and make one awkward move to gain jugs and then a ledge. Either climb through a tunnel to the top or take the rib behind the tree to the top. Discrete and fairly ancient single peg belay.
NOTE: A bolted crack line further left may give a more fitting finale to the climb, but no grade is available.

AMADEUS *** HVS 110ft
1. 70ft   5   (5a).   To the left of the south-west arête of the tower is a long groove line containing a mixture of old pegs and new bolts. This gives fine sustained bridging, passing a ledge, eventually to reach a bulge below a wide crack. If you are into limestone offwidths, thrash up this. Alternatively follow the bolts and pegs

out left to the two-bolt stance of the previous route.
2. 40ft   5   (5a).   As for CHORREOSIS.

The other three routes are located on the south face of the tower. The leftmost line is a long crack containing several ancient pegs. A selection of wires will probably be found useful.

NORMAL ** 5+ (HVS 5a) 100ft
Climb the initial crack until it fizzles out and it is possible to move right to gain a flake. Continue up a second crack (the thinner left-hand one) and over a bulge to gain the summit.

SEGOVIA *** 6a (E2 5c) 100ft
A great route up the centre of the face, perhaps the best on the mountain and not too high in the grade.
Climb easy slabs and make a tricky move to the first bolt. Continue past the smooth crux wall then follow the bolt ladder all the way to the top via sustained and mildly pumpy climbing.

AUTOPISTA * 5 (VS 4b) 80ft
The wall is bounded on the right by a water runnel capped by some strange crenellations. Bridge the groove elegantly to the summit. There is no fixed gear so a couple of slings and a few large wires for a crack near the top should be carried.

BORDILLOS DE MIJAS

Character

Mijas (pronounced Meehas) is a popular tourist town of cluttered white buildings and narrow streets in a superb setting tucked away in the hills above Fuengirola. The town is backed by lightly forested hills and overlooks the blue water of the Mediterranean. At the southern end of the town is a set of small but pleasant west-facing buttresses and a rather sombre rift in the rock that between them provide a series of generally short but worthwhile pitches. The area is very popular with the local climbers who are invariably friendly and always keen to try out their English on visitors. The climbing here lacks the grandeur of El Chorro or the magnificent isolation of El Torcal but if you are in the area the place is definitely worth a visit, and indeed connoisseurs of the short and sharp should love the place, despite its rather unkempt air. In any event a mid-winter's day climbing here is going to be vastly superior to a similar day spent splodging through the mud in deepest dankest Cheedale or blowing on chilled and wooden fingers at Tremadog.

Protection is fixed and plentiful and all routes have substantial lowering points at the top of the climbing. The actual style of climbing varies from steep and fingery to slabby and delicate and there is a broad selection of grades to go at. There is also the added advantage that the town is very close at hand if you fancy a donkey ride, buying a few Spanish knick-knacks or checking out one of the many good Tapas bars, ie. just the place for the wife (or the husband!) to go and explore while you get a few routes in. Added to this is the fact that the Mediterranean is only ten minutes drive away if your fingers give out and you fancy an afternoon paddle, or even to sample one of the many fine sea food restaurants in Fuengirola. The Versalles self-service restaurant on the sea-front is especially worth a visit if you are "on your uppers": all you can eat for 580pts, no strings attached and the food is good.

NOTE: There have been access problems here in the past and the cliff was closed to climbers for a while. A polite approach to any of the non-climbing locals who often come to watch "Los Escaladores" is probably a good idea.

Access

From Malaga follow the main coast road westwards past Torremolinos to Fuengirola.

There is an ancient British tradition of driving along this section of road with all the car windows open and singing "Here we go, here we go, here we go", at the top of your voice. This is reputed to be some Anglo Saxon mating call from pre-Moorish times and is guaranteed to mark you out as a Brit abroad.

This road is regarded as the single most dangerous piece of highway in Europe. The *Rough Guide to Spain* explains that the massive numbers of fatalities on it each years are directly attributable to foreign drivers (often inebriated) in recently collected and unfamiliar hire cars, getting into this fast and busy highway. It is not a motorway though many locals drive as if it is. This fact, coupled with pedestrians trying to cross the road and cars making U-turns, means it is a place to be on your alert. You have been warned.

Approximately eighteen kilometres from Malaga airport and just before the centre of Fuengirola there is a right turn inland signed Mijas. (There are a couple of earlier right turns that will take you more directly to Mijas but the roads are rather tortuous.) From the main coastal dual carriageway a good road climbs rapidly then a few sweeping bends bring you to the town (and the donkeys). Drive through the centre of the town following signs for the "Mercado Municipal" and taking the right fork at the only significant junction. Go past the square and on down ever narrower roads until just before the road bends away to the right to cross a small valley; the cliff is on your left. Bump down a short dirt track and park by the rocks, convenience climbing at its most accessible.

The climbs are described from left to right starting at the buttress that actually overhangs the road and is supported by a stone wall. The routes on here are generally hard and rather close together. The scruffy topos painted on the stone wall below the cliff may help you to sort the crowded geography of this buttress though I hope this guide manages that more than adequately! The convenient street lights means that climbing is possible 24 hours a day for the truly dedicated.

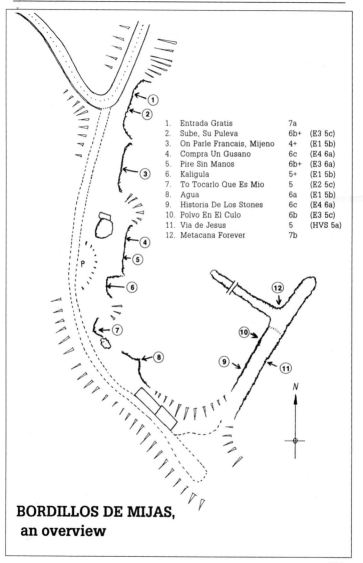

1.	Entrada Gratis	7a	
2.	Sube, Su Puleva	6b+	(E3 5c)
3.	On Parle Francais, Mijeno	4+	(E1 5b)
4.	Compra Un Gusano	6c	(E4 6a)
5.	Pire Sin Manos	6b+	(E3 6a)
6.	Kaligula	5+	(E1 5b)
7.	To Tocarlo Que Es Mio	5	(E2 5c)
8.	Agua	6a	(E1 5b)
9.	Historia De Los Stones	6c	(E4 6a)
10.	Polvo En El Culo	6b	(E3 5c)
11.	Via de Jesus	5	(HVS 5a)
12.	Metacana Forever	7b	

BORDILLOS DE MIJAS,
an overview

BORDILLOS DE MIJAS, Northern Section

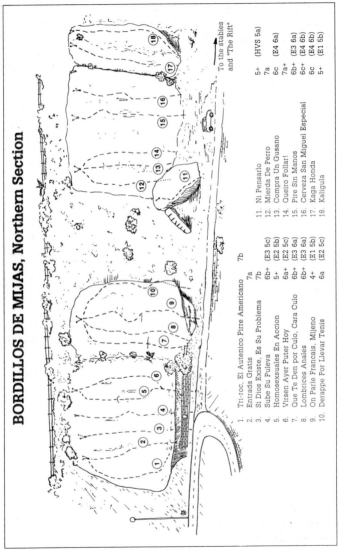

To the stables
and "The Rift"

1. Tri-roc, El Autenico Pirre Americano   7b
2. Entrada Gratis   7a
3. Si Dios Existe, Es Su Problema   7b
4. Sube Su Puleva   6b+   (E3 5c)
5. Homosexsuales En Accion   5+   (E2 5b)
6. Virsen Ayer Puter Hoy   6a+   (E2 5c)
7. Que Te Den por Culo, Cara Culo   6b+   (E3 6a)
8. Lombrices Anales   6b+   (E3 6a)
9. On Parle Francais, Mijeno   4+   (E1 5b)
10. Derappe Por Llevar Tenis   6a   (E2 5c)

11. Ni Pensarlo   5+   (HVS 5a)
12. Mierda De Perro   7a
13. Compra Un Gusano   6c   (E4 6a)
14. Queiro Follar!   7a+
15. Pire Sin Manos   6b+   (E3 6a)
16. Cerveza San Miguel Especial   6c+   (E4 6b)
17. Kaga Honda   6c   (E4 6b)
18. Kaligula   5+   (E1 5b)

LOS HIPPY NO VAN TRIPY ** 8a+ 80ft

A test of stamina. Use the bolt on hold (or spit on it) to get established on the roof then traverse left under the lip of the overhang until a particularly trying sequence takes you past the arête. With a little power left it is possible to get established on the wall above and to climb up and left to the ring bolts. Simianesque.

TRI-ROC, EL AUTENTICO PIRRE AMERICANO ** 7b 70ft

Start as for the previous route and hand traverse the lip until it is possible to pull onto the wall at twin bolts. Alternatively (and a cop out) pull straight over the roof and traverse delicately left to the twin bolts. From here follow the right side of the left arête of the buttress on tiny holds to the chains on the right.

ENTRADA GRATIS *** 7a 70ft

Pull onto the roof using the bolt on hold then power straight over into the fine shallow groove that is the main feature of this buttress. This gives technical and sustained climbing on small pockets to twin bolts with wire cables just below the cliff top.

EL MONODEDO ASESINO * 7c 70ft

From the bolt-on hold climb straight over the bulges then move up and right to more bulging rock. Continue straight up to cross the centre of the upper bulge on painful finger pockets to a final couple of easier moves.

To the right of the bolt on hold is another weakness in the overhang where some finger pockets allow access to the wall above. A rather tatty thread at twelve feet also marks the way.

SI DIOS EXISTE, ES SU PROBLEMA * 7b 70ft

Power through the initial bulges on small sharp fingerholds then climb the thin wall directly above to slightly better holds, more sustained moves on sharp pockets leads up passing to the right of the central bulges, then head off left to the chains.

Right again is an obvious break in the lower overhang where a series of large bucket holds allow a way through into the wall above. Two routes start here.

LA RUBIA DE GOMA, QUE ME LA COMA, COMA * 6c+ (E4 6a) 80ft

A rather wandering but worthwhile piece of climbing up the buttress front. Pull through the bulges on good holds then traverse left past one bolt line to the next. Move up to the bulges then swing right to join and finish up SI DIOS...

SUBE SU PULEVA ** 6b+ (E3 5c) 70ft

The direct line above the break in the overhang provides a good sustained pitch.

Pull through the bulges and climb straight up the wall until forced rightwards to better holds at some large pockets. Continue up and left now on smaller holds to reach the relatively insubstantial belays.

This route is marred slightly by the seasonal hornets nest at half height. The occupants apparently only get active once the sun has hit the rock so an alpine start might be a good idea if you are intent on doing the route without being pestered.

To the right are the last two routes on this section of the cliff. They weave their respective ways up a bizarre flowstone-covered wall and start at a break in the bulges where a set of good jugs allow access to a brand of "funny" red rock.

HOMOSEXSUALES EN ACCION ** 5+ (E2 5b) 70ft

The local certainly have a way with route names!

Pull through the bulges strenuously then step left before bucket bashing to a large undercut. The wall above proves to be rather more taxing then a short traverse right gains the chains.

VIRSEN AYER PUTER HOY * 6a+ (E2 5c) 70ft

Start as for the previous route then move right before following the steep sustained wall (on far too many pinch grips) to the belays. Quite hard for its (English) grade.

To the right is an overgrown gully and then a buttress that is basically a steep slab. This contains five pitches, four of which require a degree of delicacy and subtlety of technique. All the routes end up at the same belay so a bit of care is needed if more than one party is operating here at the same time.

QUE TE DEN POR CULO, CARA CULO * 6b+ (E3 6a) 60ft
Climb up easy overgrown ledges on the left side of the face then a short steep wall to a ledge with a peg runner down its back. The next section is rather easier than it looks thanks to a well hidden small fingerhold but the final bulge is a different beast. Once past it teeter right to the belay. The pitch was originally graded 6c, perhaps it should have been left at that.

LOMBRICES ANALES ** 6b+ (E3 6a) 50ft
Climb directly up the slab just left of the centre of the face by sustained and delicate manoeuvres. The start is precarious and rather bold, the rest is just precarious. Sneaking right on to the next route, for whatever reason, is absolutely taboo.

ON PARLE FRANÇAIS, MIJENO ** 4+ (E1 5b) 50ft
A pleasant and delicate exercise starting just to the right of the centre of the slab.

Pull awkwardly onto the slab over a bulge and climb easily to ledges. Move up and left using indifferent fingerholds and sloping footholds until it is possible to step back to the right. Continue more easily to the belays. The grades don't really add up do they?

DERRAPE POR LLEVAR TENIS * 6a (E2 5c) 60ft
A pitch of contrasts. Start under the leaning right arête of the buttress and climb its right-hand side until it is possible to pull back on the slabby face. Follow the arête above with increasing delicacy until it is possible to escape out to the left to reach the chains.

To the right is another pitch that runs straight up the leaning side wall of the buttress:

A ME DA TEUAL * 6a (E2 5c)
The severely leaning lower wall has good holds to a semi-resting ledge. The upper section leans a little less but is still hard work.

To the right past a grassy break is a quarried block apparently holding up a huge boulder. The boulder is home to four minuscule routes.

ESTO NO LO SUBE NI JAMES BOND 007a+ 20ft
The pocketed and butch underside of the boulder. Recently downgraded to 6c, but try telling your fingers that.

AZOTAME CON LA GOMA DE BUTANO 6b (E2 6a) 20ft
The leaning arête of the boulder gives a route that is marginally longer than its name.

NI PENSARLO 5+ (HVS 5a) 25ft
Diagonally left up the front face of the boulder on sharp holds then finish direct to a wire cable belay.

ESTO PAR ALCALDE 4 (VS 4c) 25ft
The right side of the front face of the boulder and the slab above to a wire cable belay.

To the right of and behind the boulder is a flat grassy area surrounded by short steep walls. Known as the SECTOR YOSEMIJAS, it provides good sunbathing and picnicking, and even a bit of fingery rock climbing.

The left side of the back wall has three short but good and challenging pitches that all end up at the same belays.

MIERDA DE PERRO * 7a 50ft
The left edge of the wall is followed on small holds and with sustained moves. Traverse right to reach the belays. The name is not a comment on the quality of the climbing.

COMPRA UN GUSANO ** 6c (E4 6a) 50ft
The shallow groove to the right of the arête is entered by some fingery pulls and followed with more of the same fare. Excellent climbing.

QUIERO FOLLAR! * 7a+ 50ft

The bulging blunt rib to the right is steep, sustained and fingery, a wearing combination. It also sports one or two slightly "improved" holds, they should have made them a bit bigger.

To the right, close to the centre of the wall is a route which is marked at the base of the cliff but at the time of writing the bolts have been removed.

To the right again and just right of the centre of the wall is a line up a section of ribbed flowstone:

PIRE SIN MANOS ** 6b+ (E3 6a) 50ft

An easy start leads to fingery and sustained moves until the angle eases. A touch more delicacy is needed to reach the chains. A pitch of subtle contrasts.

To the right a huge chain hangs from the wall. This is to replace a bolt that pulled out of a section of hollow flowstone. It provides a remarkably substantial looking running belay on the following route:

CERVEZA SAN MIGUEL ESPECIAL 6c+ (E4 6b) 50ft

Start at the beer can lid nailed to the rock.

Climb on large holds until just below the chain then continue with escalating difficulty to the top. One must assume that the remaining bolts are solid!

To the right is a narrow chimney/gully which used to await the attention of an offwidth freak with big nuts!! Such a soul has appeared and produced the neo-classical:

DIEDRO DEL "ARBOL" 4+ (VS 4c ish) 50ft

A great route if you are into thrashing up wide bush-filled cracks. Either place your own gear (very traditional, carry several Hex 10s) or clip the bolts on the slab on the right (more sensible), or avoid the route altogether (most sensible).

To the right of the deep corner is a buttress which protrudes and offers a series of good if somewhat crowded pitches.

The leftmost line of bolts on the left wall of the buttress is utilised by the previous route.

The line up the centre of this wall is:

KAGA HONDO * 6c (E4 6b) 50ft
Steep and stiff moves on funny flowstone holds lead over a "blank" bulge to gain ledges below more bulges. More steep moves on rather better holds lead to a slab and onto the chains at its very apex.

LA POLICIA ME PERSEGUIA ** 6c (E4 6a) 50ft
The arête offers a steep, sustained and technical exercise. The start is tough with the bulge being passed on small and often hidden holds and an excruciating finger jam. The upper section is a bit easier and a lot more delicate.

1,2,3 METE LANAS AL PODER * 6c+ (E4 6a) 50ft
The bulging wall just to the right of the arête has both balancy and fingery moves. Gaining the midway ledge is easiest from the right, but the upper bulge has no soft options, nicely technical.

KALIGULA ** 5+ (E1 5b) 60ft
From the base of the arête move delicately up and right into the centre of the face. This is climbed with surprising delicacy until the crux moves lead strenuously to the chains.

To the right and very close to the path is a short pinnacle block with a sharp front arête. It offers five pleasant but sadly brief pitches. To the left of the arête is:

PELEGRINO SIN DESTINO * 6a (E1 5b) 30ft
Climb the grey slabby wall keeping just left of the bolts.
Lower off. The best pitch on this buttress offering nice moves and good rock.

The arête of the block is taken by:

NI TOCARLO QUE ES MIO 5 (E2 5c) 30ft
Following the arête religiously requires a slightly myopic approach but is a technically worthwhile exercise. Clip the bolts on the previous route.
To the right of the arête are three short pitches on rugged rock.

SETE VE UN HUEVO 5+ (HVS 5a) 30ft
Climb on to a ledge to the right of the arête then continue up the wall trending rightwards on large rough holds to reach the massive belay chain. According to the name this is not a route to be done in shorts; ask a local to translate it if you don't mind being embarrassed.

COMO EL ABORTO DE UN SAPO 5+ (E1 5b) 30ft
The middle line is steeper and tougher, but the rock is just as rough and the central bulge is no pushover. The belay is shared with the previous route.

Y AHORA COMO LO HAGO 5+ (E1 5b) 30ft
The right-hand line on the wall is steeper still and becomes increasingly artificial as height is gained. It is also rather close to a very prickly bush, care required, especially if you are considering falling off.

To the right beyond some bushes the cliff swings round to face south and just a little further there is a series of low buildings. These form the accommodation for the donkeys that provide the rides in the town. The cliff here is high and impressively steep but unfortunately the foot of it is covered in...well let's just say it is no fun cleaning the soles of your boots. There are four routes here that would definitely be more highly recommended if it was not for...you know what.

ENCADENACION MOLECULAR * 6a+ (E3 5c) 80ft
Start left of the corner and climb up leftwards past a peg to a thread. Step left to a bolt then trend back right up steeply leaning rock on big but horrendously rough holds to a ledge. Cross the final bulge and reach the lowering point.

BURROS Y FRACKISS * 7a 80ft
The left wall of the central groove line is steep, strenuous and smelly.
Climb the straightforward corner then head off left up the leaning wall by sustained and strenuous climbing on pockets that are usually not quite as good as you would expect. The route deserves a better setting.

AGUA * 6a (E1 5b) 70ft
Climb the straightforward central groove until it starts to steepen up. Make a couple of wide bridging moves then swing out right to gain the arête which is followed more easily.

EXPRESSO PICALAESO * 5 (HVS 5a) 80ft
From the foot of the central corner traverse out right into a hole above the buildings. Lean round the corner to clip the first bolt (a failure on this move may give the donkey a surprise) then continue up the centre of the buttress on rugged rock and good holds.

Around to the right of the buildings a path leads up a short steep bank and into an impressive rift in the ground that was quarried in antiquity. This is the:

Sector le Raja de Mijas

The rift contains a series of steep and worthwhile pitches that are sometimes rather dusty. As a climbing venue the place is a bit gloomy though it is a suitable venue in high summer or for refugees from Huntsman's Leap who are suffering withdrawal symptoms. The quality of the climbing and the interesting nature of the rock makes up somewhat for the shortcomings of the setting. The sun shines into the rift for a couple of hours shortly after midday, illuminating it with golden glow and dispelling the gloom.

At the time of writing considerable development was going on here, and it is reassuring to know that the bolts being placed in the rather "unusual" rock were of a substantial length.

The area above the rift is a public park, so it is probably a good idea to keep a weather eye open in case any of the day trippers try to find how deep the hole is by throwing things down it.

The routes are described first from left to right on the left wall, and then from right to left on the right wall, ie. as they are passed when you walk into the rift.

The Left Wall

HISTORIA DE LOS STONES ** 6c (E4 6a) 90ft
A good route quite low in the grade with a climax high on the wall.
Climb the leaning lower section with sustained moves on good
holds until a welcome ledge can be reached. Step right and climb the
upper wall on spaced holds passing an unhelpful diagonal crack to
reach the chains.

AY! QUE DESVIRGUE ** 6b+ (E3 5c) 90ft
Start to the left of a pile of rubble and climb up leftwards to the first
bolt. Continue past an amazing fossil-filled pocket then bear right
up the fine sustained upper wall on holds which are generally good
but are often rather spaced.

To the right of the pile of rubble and to the left of the "dry stone
wall" that crosses the rift are two pitches that start in the same place.

OHO QUE CHUNGO *** 80ft 6c (E4 6a)
A magnificent pitch, perhaps the best in the rift.
A leaning start on spaced but good holds leads to marginally
easier angled rock, unfortunately the holds decrease in size and are
often well hidden so the interest is well maintained. A bulging
section is passed on small "flatties" and the upper wall is just run
out enough to add a touch of spice.

POLVO EN EL CULO ** 80ft 6b (E3 5c)
Start as for the previous route to the first bolt then hand traverse to
the right (a direct start is possible but is a bit dusty) before climbing
steeply into the base of the fine scoop in the upper section of the cliff.
Step left onto the wall and weave your way up this to the top by
sustained moves.

The next two routes are found by scrambling past the dry stone
wall that crosses the rift to an impressive arête on the left. They both
start by traversing out onto the left wall from here.

DESVIRGADA *** 5+ (E1 5b) 100ft

Climb the arête a short distance then traverse out to the left passing below a leaning red groove containing a line of bolts. Step up then continue round the corner to reach the foot of a superb open scoop in the upper wall. This is followed with sustained interest to a steep and exposed exit on the right to reach the ledges at the top of the rift. Twin-bolt belay then abseil back in from the railings.

ESPAGHETTI Y ACEITUNA ** E4 80ft

1. 50ft   6b   (5c).   Start as for the previous route but climb the steep, red groove with sustained interest and on mostly good holds to reach a flat ledge and twin-bolt belay below the tilted prow that crowns the wall.
2. 30ft   6c   (6a).   Climb the leaning wall close to its left edge to a strenuous exit. Impressive stuff, especially from where the second is stood.

The Right Wall

This next set of routes is described as they are passed when walking into the rift.

The first route starts a short way in from daylight where there is a prominent flat ledge at ten feet.

BEAT ESKALA BEIN * 5+ (E1 5b) 40ft

Climb up to the ledge and some post holes then zigzag up the steep wall on good but spaced pockets. Quite a steep little pitch!

Fifteen metres further into the rift is a classic climb, easily identifiably as such because of the polished nature of its holds:

VIA DE JESUS *** 5 (HVS 5a) 80ft

Climb the lower wall to a bay then continue to make steep moves into and out of a niche, fortunately the jugs are impressive both in size and frequency. Easier climbing leads to the chains.

Eight metres left again two routes start together:

CACA EN EL CULO ** 6a (E2 5b) 80ft

Up easily to ledges then straight up to the steep sustained wall on good pockets until a ledge can be gained. Move left then finish direct.

VUELOS IBERIA ** 6b (E3 5c) 80ft

Start just left of the previous pitch and climb easily to a large round hole. Follow the steep flake to reach good pockets on the right at the base of a shallow groove. Swing left onto the leaning face then climb to a ledge and on awkwardly to the top.

The last area is "the inner sanctum" where two impressively steep pitches are to be found. Cross the dry stone wall and scramble into the cave-like recess where the rift splits into two.

The impressive hanging arête dead ahead is:

METACANA FOREVER *** 7a+ 70ft

Climb steeply up to the right then follow the leaning arête with powerful moves between chiefly good holds on rock set at an angle that is not quite (but very nearly) ridiculous. Just below the top is a sloping ledge often occupied by pigeons, be warned when they are absent their "presents" linger on.

The final route is found by scrambling up the left fork until just beyond the foot bridge spanning the gap high overhead. The right wall here has a strip of solid red rock taken by:

TUBERCULO HERECFUY ** 7a 60ft

More leaning jug pulling, an escape from the pit back into the sunny land of the living. If you make it, lower back in for more of the same.

Another small collection of cliffs has been developed at Mijas. They may be of value if the main area is crowded or you have done every route there and are still hungering for more.

Sector la Ermita

When driving up the main road just before Mijas there is a right turn to Benalmadena, opposite a large petrol station. Follow this for 0.9 kilometres to a right turn sign La Ermita. This road leads to a chapel after only 300 metres. Close to here there are two sections that have been developed so far. For the first one park at the chapel and follow a vague track around to the right of the chapel gate passing a strange collection of statues. After 100 metres or so there is a large west-facing cave on the left that contains three good looking and exceptionally steep routes up to eighty feet high, a suitable venue for jug jockeys, pump it up.

For the second area drive past the chapel and on down a white concrete road. Part way down this is a track on the right with a wire cable across it. Park here and follow the track for 100 metres to an impressive quarried hole cutting deeply into the hillside. Above this is an east-facing wall up to sixty feet high with six routes that appear to be in the HVS to E2 range, and with a rather harder pitch on the left.

OTHER AREAS

There is considerable scope for development along the Costa del Sol and inland from the coast. Discussion with the locals has led me to a couple of places that are in the early stages of development and are worth visiting if you are in the area, but at present are not really worth a trip from afar.

Benhavis

A small collection of routes of a variety of grades situated in a quiet valley six kilometres inland from the coast. From Malaga drive down the main coast road through Torremolinos, Fuengirola and Marbella to San Pedro: fifty-seven kilometres from Malaga, thirty-three kilometres from Fuengirola. On leaving San Pedro there is a minor right turn signed to Benhavis. This is followed for six kilometres to a point where the valley narrows and there is parking available on the right. On the other side of the river (which contains some pretty mean swimming hollows) is an impressive leaning streak wall that is undeveloped at present but could provide plenty of sport the wrong side of vertical. Further to the left is a shorter but still steep wall that has a number of worthwhile pitches on it. The other area that has been developed lies a steep five-minute scramble up the bank on the other side of the road.

The rock has a rather strange appearance and is in fact a form of marble with blackened surface. Holds and friction are excellent and all the routes are bolt-protected. They vary from 20 feet to 120 feet in height. The first couple of routes are on the underside of some large boulders on the right of the approach path, they are short and very steep. On the left side of the main crag is a black slabby wall with a couple of pleasant climbs about grade 5 (HVS), whilst to the right across a gully are some rather steeper pitches up to 6c (E3 6a). Next comes a huge deep rift with a boulder jammed in its throat and a "super route" on its gently leaning left wall. Right again are two short but steep pitches, one a groove and one a rib leading to ledges. From these an easier pitch leads up the fine face to the top of the buttress.

Manilva

A collection of short and mostly easy routes on the edge of a limestone plateau peppered with towers, minarets and pagodas; the plateau is well worth exploring. The rock is excellent and the protection is fixed.

The cliff is reached by driving down the coast road through Marbella, San Pedro and Estapona. Ten kilometres past the last of these is a right turn signed to Manilva which is reached in two kilometres (seventy kilometres from Fuengirola). Drive through the town and follow the road to a quarry which is skirted on the left (the impressive cliff beyond the quarry is untouched at present). Continue uphill then along a level road for a couple of kilometres to a left turn signed to a racing track. Turn right here down a narrow road, pass in front of a farm and go through a wire gate to parking on the right, opposite where an old track branches off to the left. Follow this track for a couple of hundred metres until it doubles back then continue straight on to find the Lower Tier just up to the left.

This band of rock contains about a dozen routes mostly 3 (Severe) to 5 (HVS 5a), but with a couple of toughies on the left. Continuing along the same level is a scattering of routes and a lot of unclimbed rock with some obvious steep challenges.

Above this Lower Tier is another band of cliffs that is rather more impressive, again this is only lightly developed with MAGREO VERTICAL (6c (E4 6a) on the left and three easier routes around a square pinnacle. The groove is ALLA LANTOTA (Diff), the rib on its right is CHUMBASCH (Severe) and the front face of the pinnacle is PABRE BONSAI * 4 (VS 4b). Some walls several hundred metres away to the right also contain a few climbs.

On the opposite (shady) side of the valley is a series of grey walls that contain a small selection of short routes.

Twenty-five kilometres down the road is a great big rock that sticks out into the sea, it might be worth a visit. I think the locals call it Gibraltar. Just across the water is another Africa, there is probably a bit to do there as well.

TENERIFE

NOTE: I am aware that Tenerife is not actually part of Andalusia, but as there is nothing else written in English about the rock climbing in this very popular holiday destination, I thought a few brief pointers might be of use to anybody visiting the island for the first time. If the inclusion of Tenerife upsets your sensibilities please feel free to remove the following pages.

Introduction

Tenerife is the largest of the Canary Islands, with the whole group sometimes being known as the Fortunate Islands or the Islands of Eternal Spring. There exists a small nucleus of climbers living on the island and in recent years Spaniards from the mainland have been going to Tenerife to escape the winter cold ("cold" of course being a relative term).

As a winter holiday venue the place has a lot to offer, being only 400 miles north of the tropics. In fact the surrounding ocean and the prevailing north-east trade winds means that the weather is remarkably constant throughout the whole year, with daytime temperatures in the seventies and eighties, and little in the way of rain, especially on the southern half of the island. The place therefore makes an ideal holiday destination at any time of the year, especially if getting a tan is part of your sports plan. The almost continuous but highly predictable winds have led to Tenerife being one of the world centres for wind surfing. If you always fancied a go but could not face the prospect of falling into Lyn Padarn or Coniston Water, then here's your chance with no excuses. It is also a great spot for on- and off-road mountain biking. Most airlines will carry your bike free of charge as long as it is properly packed, check with them if you fancy the thought of a change from cycling in the rain and/or traffic.

The whole island chain is of volcanic origin and there is still plenty of evidence in the form of lava fields, cinder cones and great areas of ash; in fact the main volcano (El Tiede) last erupted in 1909 and so on a geological time scale the place is still well and truly active. Exploring the most recently active areas is to take a trip into

149

another world: don't forget your camera. The ascent of the volcano is a worthwhile day out, the ice-clad summit slopes complete with holes belching sulphurous steam guaranteeing a fun ending to a long trip. (Using the cable-car is definitely taboo if you want to get the full tick, but then again you are on holiday.) In several areas the basalt plateaux that form large sections of the island have been heavily dissected and spectacular ravines up to 3,000 feet deep offer superb walking and scrambling in dramatic settings. These usually start from the road that encircles the island and end up at sea level. With a bit of forethought it is possible to arrange to have a boat to meet you, the alternative being a reversal of the downward trip.

There are several walking guides that describe these and other outings, and these can be bought either in the UK or on the island.

How to get there, when to go and where to stay

As mentioned in the introduction all the Canary Islands offer year round settled weather, though it is the guarantee of winter sunshine that makes the archipelago such a popular destination. Unlike the other areas in this book Tenerife is well geared up to the mass tourist industry and all this entails. On the plus side there are frequent cheap flights all year round and plenty of inexpensive accommodation on the island. On the downside there is the classic Brits abroad syndrome; English bars, Watney's Red Barrel, loud discos, and red-faced lager louts, a far cry from the fastnesses of Andalusia, but then again variety is the spice of life!

Tenerife is a very popular holiday destination throughout the winter because of the climate, and can be pricey especially over the Christmas period, though much cheaper at other times. There are plenty of "all in" packages available with flights from all UK regional airports. Alternatively it is possible to book a flight only, try any travel agent or one of the numbers on Oracle on the TV. There is plenty of accommodation available - apartments, villas and hotels - to suit most pockets. Magazines such as *Owners Abroad* or *Dalton's Weekly* should give you more than enough choice. Any of the "concrete in the desert" resorts on the south side of the island would be a good base but it is probably worth avoiding Playa de las Americas unless you are into nightlife in a big way. If you do end up here the Octopus water park costs £7 a day but is worth it, the

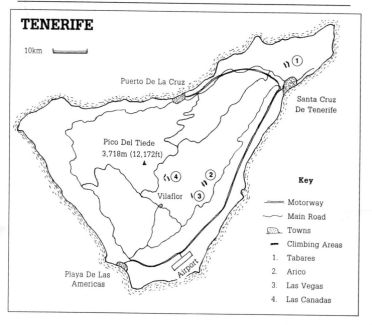

TENERIFE

10km

Puerto De La Cruz

Santa Cruz
De Tenerife

Pico Del Tiede
3,718m (12,172ft)
▲

Vilaflor

Key

═══ Motorway

‿ Main Road

Towns

▬ Climbing Areas

1. Tabares
2. Arico
3. Las Vegas
4. Las Canadas

Playa De Las
Americas

Airport

biggest chutes will give you a buzz at least as great as soloing a grit
E5! The resorts on the north side of the island are a bit remote from
most of the climbing but are much more pleasant places to stop; it
hinges mainly on the kind of holiday you are after. Of course
camping and/or bivouacking are possible, with the weather less
extreme than on most alpine routes! Tenerife is a great place to start
your career as a beach bum, though there is a problem with easily
accessible drinking water, especially in the hills.

Hiring a car is virtually essential as the cliffs are well scattered
and in quite remote areas. It is probably best to avoid major
companies such as Hertz and Avis who charge over £200 a week,
instead try Premier Car Hire (0279 641040) or Holiday Autos (071
491 1111), who will do you a "cheap and cheerful" car for about £90
a week. Roof racks or child seats can normally be fitted free of
charge.

Food and drink are slightly more expensive than in mainland

Spain though still cheaper than back home. Due to low taxes, luxury items such as watches, cameras etc. are particularly cheap, especially if you are prepared to do a bit of bartering. Do your homework, know what you are looking for and how much you are prepared to pay and you can make a real killing.

The Climbing

Four main areas have been developed and they are quite different in atmosphere, setting and style of climbing. Bolt-protection is the norm, although occasional pegs are in place as well. A selection of wires/Friends would not go amiss especially on the easier climbs, and on the crack lines at TABARES (see below). If you get fed up with, or are not into, sport climbing there is enough rock to go and have a lifetime of adventures on, and a lot of it looks very good. The four main areas are described from north to south (see map).

Tabares

The most popular cliff on Tenerife, but only because it is situated almost amongst the outskirts of Santa Cruz, the largest city on the island, and home of most of the climbing community. The rock is a columnar basalt, rather blocky and with a mixture of both face routes and some fine cracks. There are two cliffs, a popular smaller one where a lot of top roping goes on and the routes are generally easier, and a large crag with tough bolt-protected face routes and some fine straight-sided crack lines that require the use of nuts or small Friends, again top roping is pretty much the norm.

The crag is reached by following the road (not the motorway) between Santa Cruz and La Laguna for three kilometres to the town of La Cuesta. A right turn (northwards) along a minor road passes some army barracks and then after a couple of kilometres swings round left to cross a ravine. This is where the climbing is to be found with the small wall (Pared Pequena) below the road and the larger (Pared Grande, up to thirty metres high) on the opposite side of the ravine. Although the small cliff is the most popular the best routes are on the larger ones.

On the Pared Pequena is a series of grooves and on the left are a couple of short test pieces at about 7a. To the right the first groove is VIA DEL NIDO 5+ (E1 5b), whilst the next one is DIEDRO DESVIRGADO at the same grade. The arête that bounds this groove is EL ESPOLON 6a+ (E2 5c) then there is yet another groove followed by MACROCALMA 5+ (E1 5b). The face further right is climbed by SOPA DE TRIPIS 6b+ (E3 6a) and starting at a lower level are the obvious lines of LA MURCIELAGO and DIEDRE YABLONSKI, both of which are 5+ (E1 5b).

The Pared Grande is split by a ledge at quarter height and this is most easily reached by abseil from any of the belay bolts above the wall. There are over twenty routes on this face and many of them are of a high standard. The climbs tend to either follow striking crack lines (6a to 6c) containing little in the way of fixed gear, or the smooth faces between the cracks. The latter group of routes are bolt-protected and generally tough to very tough (7a to 7c), though in fact many of both the crack and the face routes are top roped a lot more often than they are led. The actual geography of the face is rather confusing with a series of similar looking grooves and crack lines, the simplest way to sort the place out is to collar one of the locals. They are invariably friendly and most speak at least a smattering of English. When you are totally pooped it is only fifteen minutes drive to the magnificent beach at la Playa de Teresitas, a short distance north of Santa Cruz. Most of Tenerife's beaches are dark because of the volcanic rock that they have been eroded from. This particular beach is brilliant white for the simple reason that the whole thing was imported from Western Sahara, 250 miles away over the horizon.

Arico

A very pleasant open gorge where the rock is an ignibrite or welded tuff. This was blasted from the volcano during an eruption and was so hot on landing that it fused together to form a hard rough rock peppered with pockets. The rock is similar to that at the world famous Smith Rock of Oregon, though unfortunately it is only up to about eighty feet high. Face routes predominate, with plenty of

Chris Craggs on an un-named but typical pockety wall 6a (E2 5c), on the west side of the Arico ravine

limestone-like pocket pulling, up vertical and leaning walls. Routes vary in grade from 5 (HVS) to 7b+, with the majority of the climbs in the 6a to 7a range. There are about a hundred pitches here on walls that face both east and west, so it is therefore possible to climb in, or avoid, the sun depending on the temperature and your temperament. There is also a lower ravine that has about twenty hard routes and a lot of very steep and undeveloped rock. Don't forget to pack your drill.

The cliff lies above the village of Val de Arico (called Lomo de Arico on some maps) which is on the old road from Santa Cruz to Los Cristianos, about thirty-five kilometres north of the latter. Turn uphill in the centre of Val de Arico and follow the road round the church and past a most bizarre tree. Continue for 2.4 kilometres, passing two sets of hairpins until a track branches right just before some white houses. Follow this (OK in a hire car!) for half a kilometre to parking by two big trees. Descend into the ravine by a pipe and walk upstream to the climbing. The lower gorge is five minutes walk in the other direction.

There are routes on both sides of the gorge, most of the better ones being on the left (western) side. Those on the right side tend to be short and sharp though the longer line of green bolts that marks the route LA VENGANZA DEL GODO 6b+ (E3 5c) is worth seeking out. Behind a group of pine trees on the left side are some short leaning walls and further right a fine steep, slab home of NELSON MANDELE (he gets around) 5+ (E1 5b). Further right a steep wall is tackled by PLACA DE FRIKI 6b+ (E3 6a), a great pitch with a fingery start and a delicate upper slab offering a climb of contrasts. Further up the valley is a whole series of routes in the Sectors Pena del Lunes and Juancho. These are generally on vertical or slightly leaning pillars of rock, and involve sharp pocket pulling, mostly graded 6b to 7a, take your pick.

Below this area in the centre of the ravine is a giant boulder whose steep side contains one of the area's harder problems; LAGARTO JUANCHO 7c+, a series of (unnatural?) finger pockets up a very leaning face.

Las Vegas

Another cliff of basalt, with about thirty routes graded mostly in the 6s (E2 to E4). This the least worthwhile of the developed cliffs, a bit loose and dusty, but is worth a visit if you are in the area.

It is reached by turning uphill in the centre of the village of Chimiche (signed Las Vegas) and following the road for three kilometres until it fizzles out. The village is rather less grand than its Nevada namesake! Follow the track uphill for about ten minutes until there is another track branching down to the left. This is followed over a dry gulch, through some orange orchards (light refreshments) and up to the left side of the cliff behind some pine trees. This left-hand section has about ten short routes mostly 6a to 6c (E1 to E4) and the desperate leaning arête of KILMA 7b+. Further right across a field of prickly pears is the Sector Moco. The routes here are higher, and are mostly 6a to 6c with a couple of harder offerings. According to the Spanish magazine there is another cliff an hours walk up the valley called El Risco del Muerto, containing about a dozen routes from 5+ (E1) to 7c. I have not made it there yet, though the place could be worth a visit.

Las Canadas

Las Canadas means The Ravines and the climbing is centred around Las Canadas del Capricho, or the Canyons of Whim, so-called because of the bizarre or whimsical rock formations encountered in this area. It is the premier climbing area on the island with around 200 routes in a brilliant and out-of-this-world setting. The rock is a pale breccia that looks loose until you rub your nose against it, at which point it turns out to be extremely solid, with a similar feel to the best of Gogarth. From the cliff the perfectly formed Fuji-like cone of El Tiede glistens with its winter coat of snow, and blocky scoria lava fields wrap themselves around the foot of the cliff. Although at an altitude of nearly 8,000 feet climbing is possible in shorts or lightweight tracksuits and T shirts throughout the winter. The thin air is inclined to produce a bit of puffing and panting but also allow for rapid sun tanning. Despite this the conditions on the shady side of the cliff can be bitter, with iron-hard snow patches showing no signs of melting through into the spring. These areas would doubtless be a great venue in high summer to escape the heat.

To reach the climbing area follow any of the roads that lead up towards El Tiede. At the pass of the Boca de Tauce (about one hour from the coast) head west until the road rises through an area of strange blue rock.

NOTE: To the left at this point is a fine series of towers (Las Catedrals) running away up the hill and about fifteen minutes walk from the car. There are many routes here up to 300 feet high on good rock. There is little in the way of fixed gear so take a full rack, double ropes and some abseil slings, a good time is assured.

As the road levels out there is a right turn signed "Los Roques". This is followed for a couple of hundred metres to parking by a small building.

Right behind the building is a fine set of pale slabs that offer many routes from V. Diff to HVS, though there is very little in the way of fixed gear, apart from the occasional bolt runner or belay. Take a few wires and enjoy yourself.

Passing around to the left of these slabs you come across the best developed part of the cliff in the form of a deep bay with a fine south-facing wall. In the back of the bay is a series of short but very overhanging pitches many of which utilise what a Spanish magazine euphemistically described as "carved clutches". The toughest route here is ANDRES PRUEBALA OTRA VEZ at 8a, crossing the widest part of the roofs, and there are several easier offerings, all of which are well protected.

The north side of the bay is the Sector Cardero, a place that always appears to be in the sun. This is a fine wall thirty metres high and split by a series of thin diagonal cracks. There are approximately a dozen routes on this face and all are well worthwhile. On the far left is the smooth face of HANKY PUNKY 7b while to the right of an easy diagonal crack is the steep, shallow groove of CUAJADA DE PUS 6c (E3 5c), offering sustained climbing to a prominent large lowering bolt. Right again is another shallow groove reached by a steep wall, TRANSILVANIA 6b+ (E3 6a). The lower pockety wall is probably the crux but the groove itself is a right grovel, passing several peg runners. The last major line on the wall is UNEQUILIBRIO 7a with a bold crux section above paired bolts. To the right is a series of shorter climbs the best of which is the innocuous looking slanting crack of AMARILLO 6b (E2 5b). The left edge of this main face contains a superb corner groove, CARDERO 3 (Severe) that leads to the summit of the tower in two pitches of classical corner and face climbing. A tricky descent is possible down the short side of the tower. The face around to the left contains at least a couple of fine slab routes that weave through bulges at E1/2.

Beyond and to the left of the Sector Cardero is a maze of pinnacles, bays and hollows: the Sector Aureola, containing thirty or so routes of all grades. It is well worth a visit but only gets the sun late on in the day in the depths of winter. Round behind this area is the spectacular twenty-metre overhanging beak of the Techo de Madrid with three upside down routes that cross it from 7c to 8a+, Batmen only need apply and don't forget your "batsuckers".

Returning to the initial slabs in front of the car park, but running away right are series of towers and walls with a whole collection of shortish routes in a sunny aspect. The most right-hand of these is the Sector Guiri with several routes on its south-east side. The central bulging wall with only two bolts, at HVS 5a and the leaning groove in the arête of the tower, GUIRI 6c (E4 6a) are the best here. Behind this is the double tower that forms the Sectors Quisqui and Chomino. There are thirty or so routes here from 4 to 8a facing in all directions. The fine white slab that forms the impressive front face of the first tower is especially worth seeking out and goes at the remarkably reasonable grade of 5 (HVS 5a).

Up the hill from the last area is the prominent crenellated tower of Fraguel Rock with a dozen climbs on a couple of fine faces and through some very impressive overhangs. On the left the big roofs are breached by (left to right) PUSI 6b (E3 5c), COSI 6a (E2 5c) and MUSI 6c (E4 6a), all involving wild swinging on large holds up very steep rock. The smooth face on the right is scaled, at least by the talented, via the route DUDO 7b+ (E6 6b).

Even further up the hill is the impressive leaning red wall of the Sector Rainbow with the ever-tilting ladder of jugs that is the RAINBOW itself 6a (E2 5b), it is well worth the walk up. To the left are two other lines just as steep but with rather less generous holds; on the left is TOTOPANI 6c+ (E4 6a) and on the right CHAPITA LEJENA 6b+ (E3 5c).

APPENDIX

Timetable for trains from Malago to El Chorro

MALAGA	8.40	10.40	12.00	13.15	13.45	15.55
ALORA	9.21	11.05	12.40	13.55	14.23	16.36
EL CHORRO	9.37	-	-	-	14.38	-

MALAGA	17.10	17.45	18.05	19.35	21.22	21.45
ALORA	17.38	18.24	18.43	20.20	22.05	22.15
EL CHORRO	-	-	-	20.51	-	-

Timetable for trains from El Chorro to Malaga

EL CHORRO	7.20	-	-	-	-	15.30
ALORA	7.37	8.54	9.53	13.00	14.25	15.52
MALAGA	8.21	9.30	10.30	13.40	15.10	16.32

EL CHORRO	-	-	20.08
ALORA	16.50	18.28	20.23
MALAGA	17.32	19.00	21.05

Ticket price (spring 1991)
Day return: Malaga to El Chorro   360pts
              Malaga to Alora   300pts

Printed by Carnmor Print & Design
95/97 London Road, Preston